Alfred's Basic Piano Li

Musical Concepts Book
Level 3

Theory Worksheets and Solos

This MUSICAL CONCEPTS BOOK reviews and reinforces the most important musical and theoretical concepts introduced in LESSON BOOK 3 of Alfred's Basic Piano Library. Each of the 11 units included consists of a two-page theoretical explanation and worksheet on a specific concept, plus a two-page solo that demonstrates the concept in an attractive musical setting. As all material is new and different from LESSON BOOK 3 and THEORY BOOK 3, the book serves as a valuable and important follow-up in aiding the student to better understand the most important musical concepts being presented.

Instructions for Use

1. MUSICAL CONCEPTS BOOK 3 may be used *after* the student completes LESSON BOOK 3. Used in this way, the book serves as an excellent review of the most important new concepts, while giving the student some additional time before continuing with LESSON BOOK 4.
2. MUSICAL CONCEPTS BOOK 3 may also be used *simultaneously* with LESSON BOOK 3 and THEORY BOOK 3, serving as excellent reinforcement of the most important new concepts at the same time they are being introduced. When used in this manner, assignments are ideally made according to the instructions on the upper right corner of the first page of each unit.
3. Finally, this MUSICAL CONCEPTS BOOK may be used with *any* piano method at a time selected by the teacher. Whichever way this series is used, the student is given an additional opportunity to learn the important and sometimes complex concepts being taught.

Martha Mier • June C. Montgomery

Cover illustration and interior art by Christine Finn

Unit 1

Use after Alfred's Basic Piano Library LESSON BOOK 3, page 7.

An Extended Position

An EXTENDED POSITION contains notes that go beyond the five-finger position.

Five-finger Position

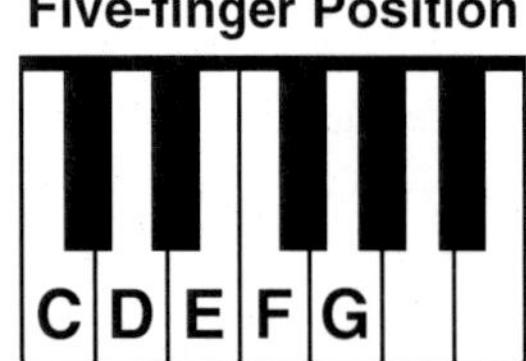

Extended Position

C E G C

RH 1 2 3 5
LH 5 4 2 1

G MAJOR

Five-finger Position

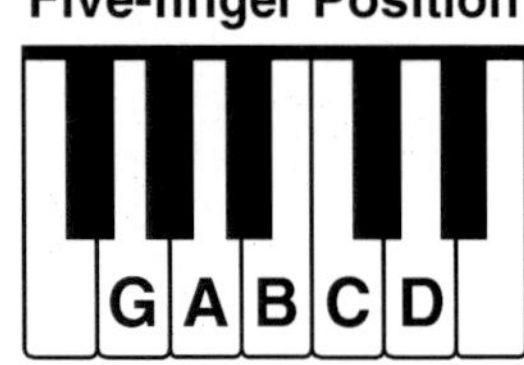

Extended Position

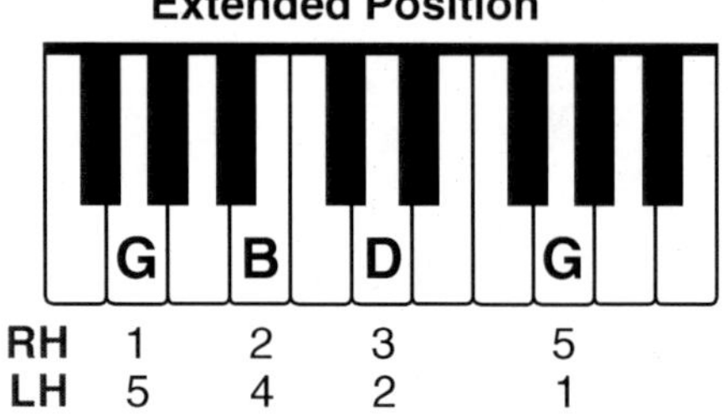

D MAJOR

Five-finger Position

Extended Position

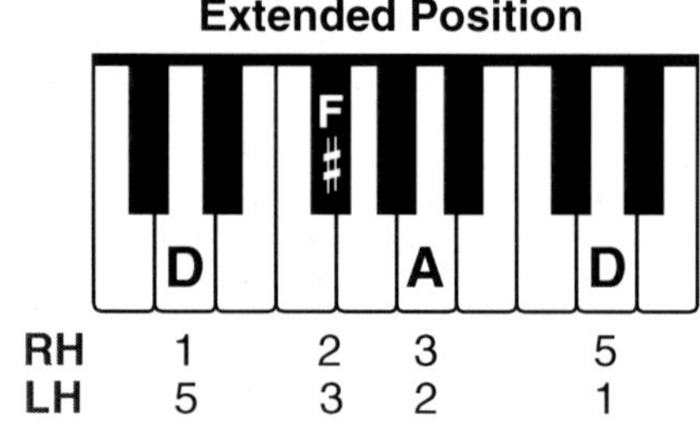

Are the examples below in a FIVE-FINGER POSITION or an EXTENDED POSITION?
Circle the correct answer. Play each example.

1\. 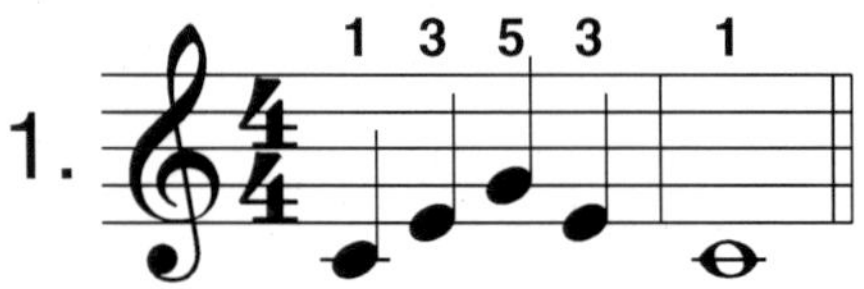

Five-finger Position

Extended Position

2\. 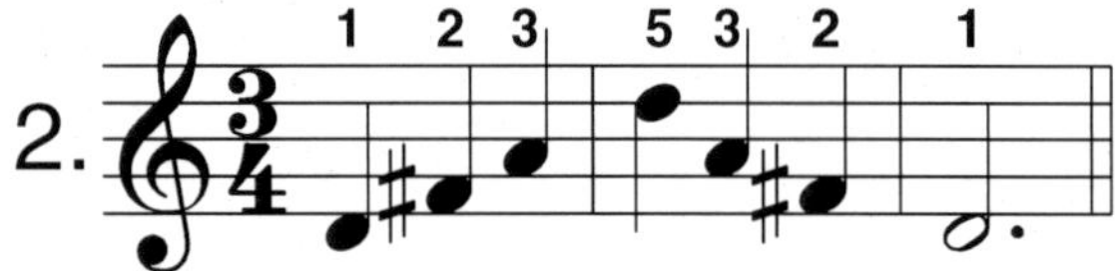

Five-finger Position

Extended Position

3\. 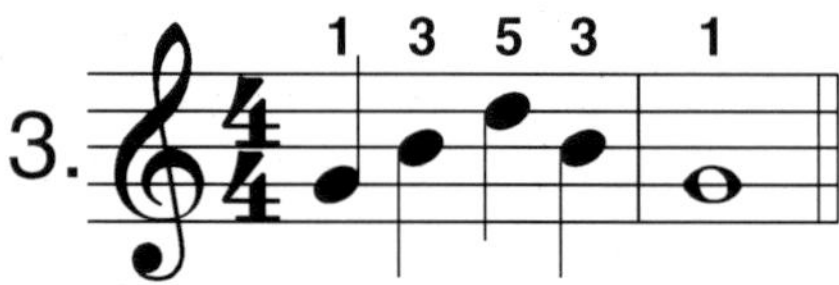

Five-finger Position

Extended Position

4\. 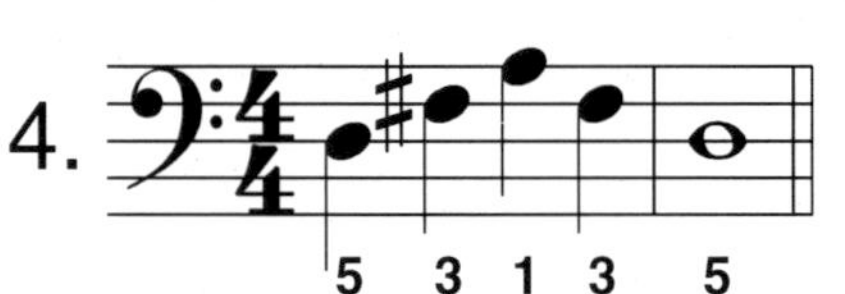

Five-finger Position

Extended Position

5\.

5 4 2 1 2 4 5

Five-finger Position

Extended Position

6\. 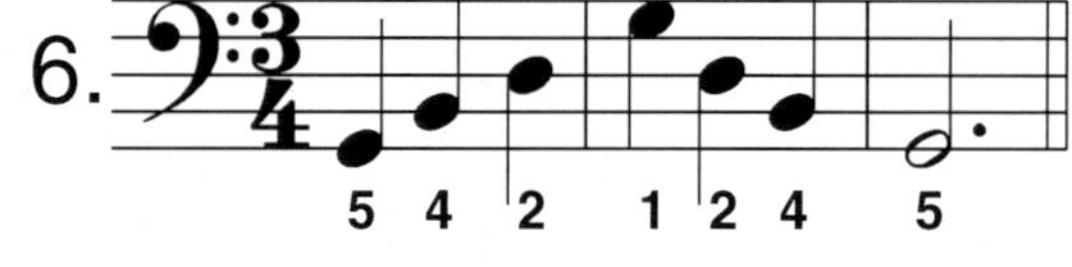

Five-finger Position

Extended Position

On the lines under the staff, write the letter names of the notes. Play each example.

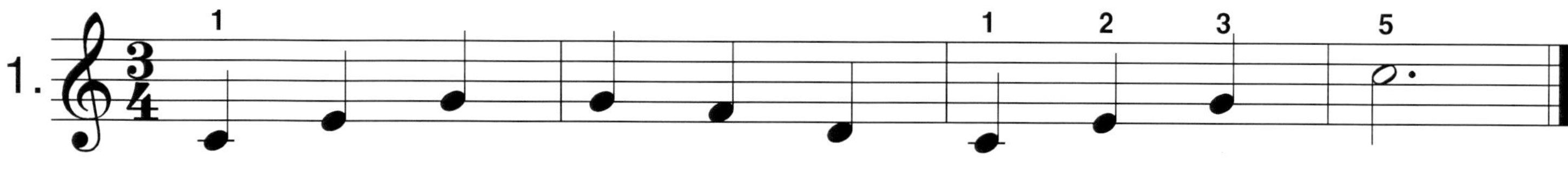

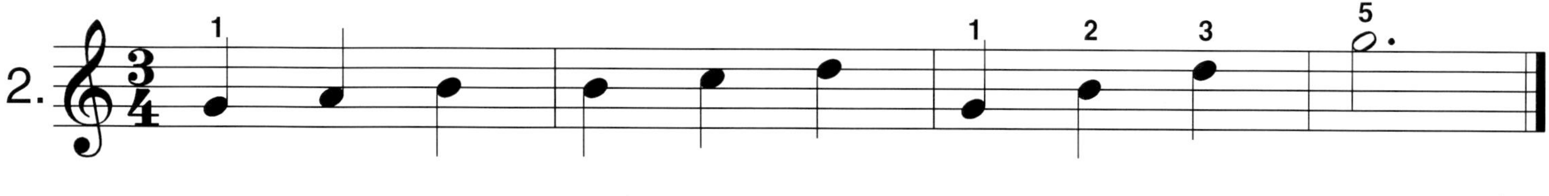

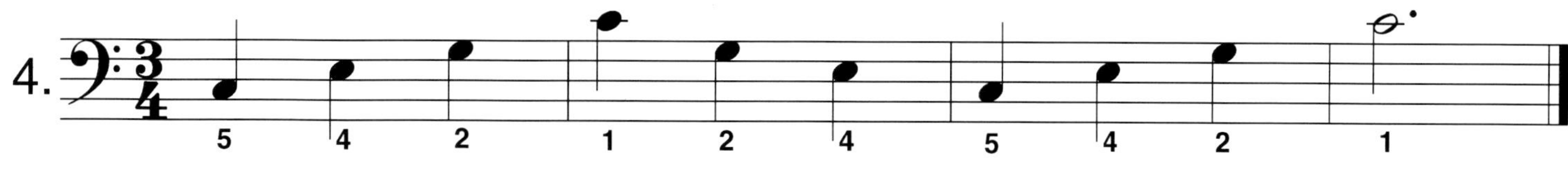

Draw a line from each extended position to its correct note names.

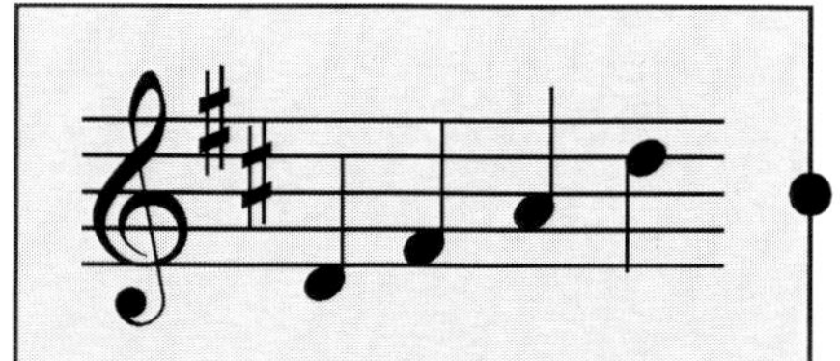

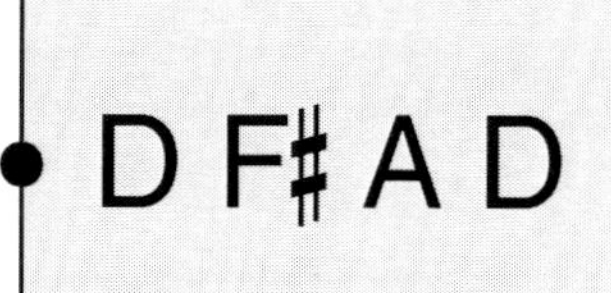

Sweet Betsy from Pike

Circle each extended position in the RH of *SWEET BETSY FROM PIKE.*

Traditional
Arr. by Martha Mier

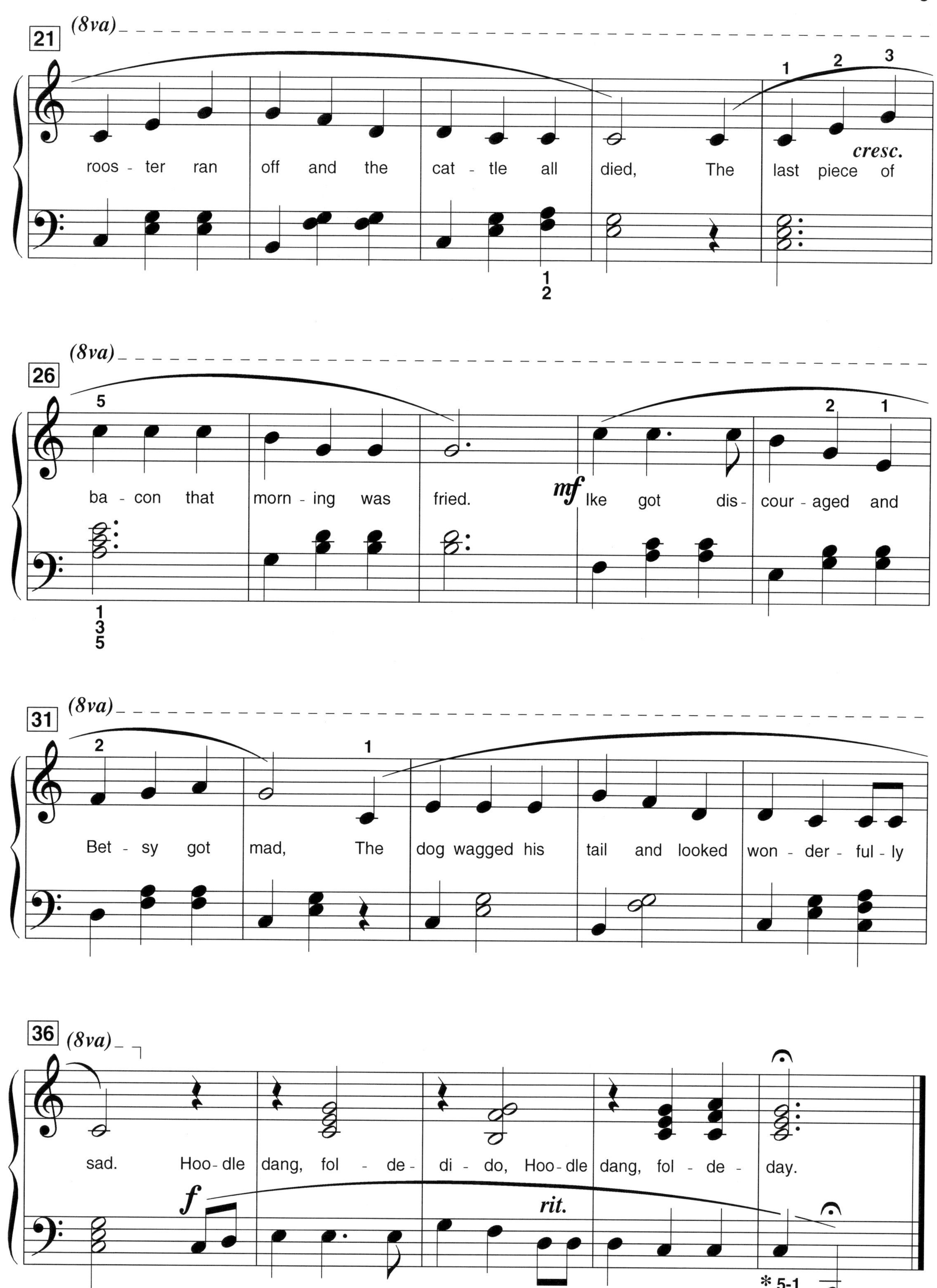

* FINGER SUBSTITUTION: While holding the note down with 5, change to 1.

Unit 2

Use after page 9.

Primary Chords—Review

BLOCK CHORDS

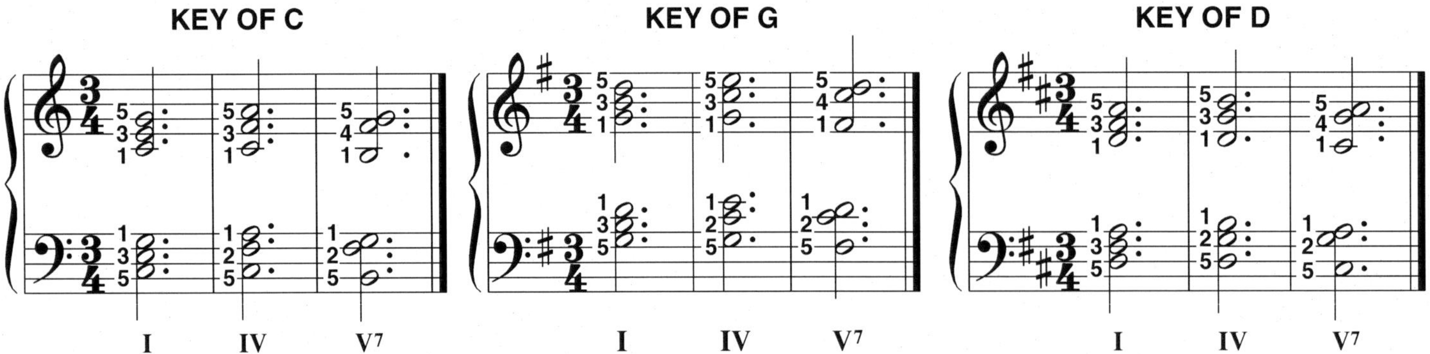

BROKEN CHORDS

Using broken chords, fill in the empty staff in each measure by writing the notes of the indicated primary chords. On the lines below the staff, write the letter name of each note.

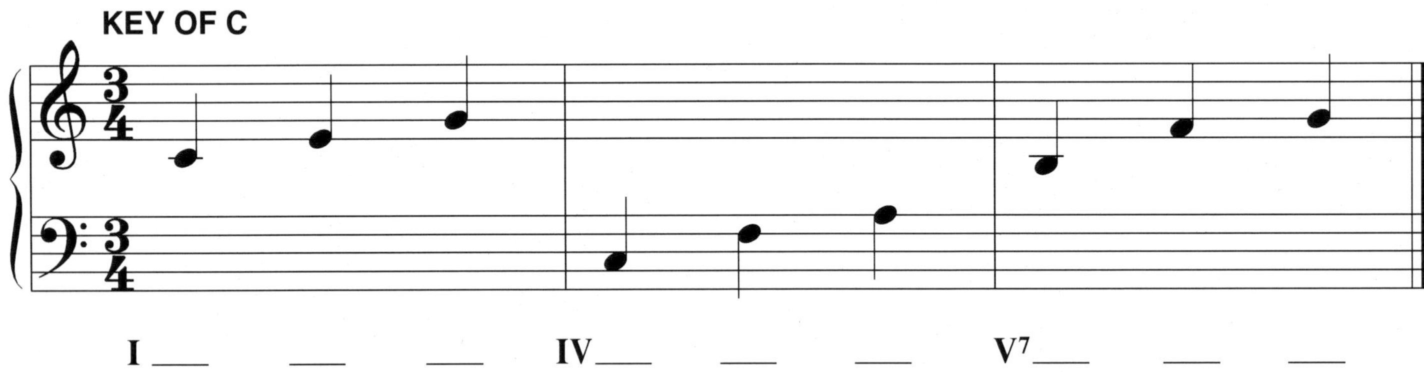

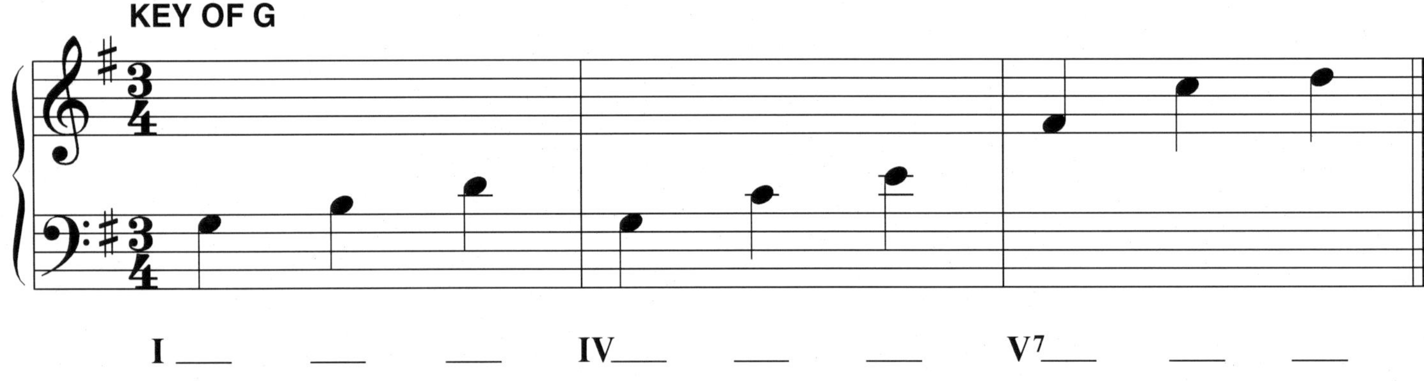

Draw a line from each chord to its correct key name.

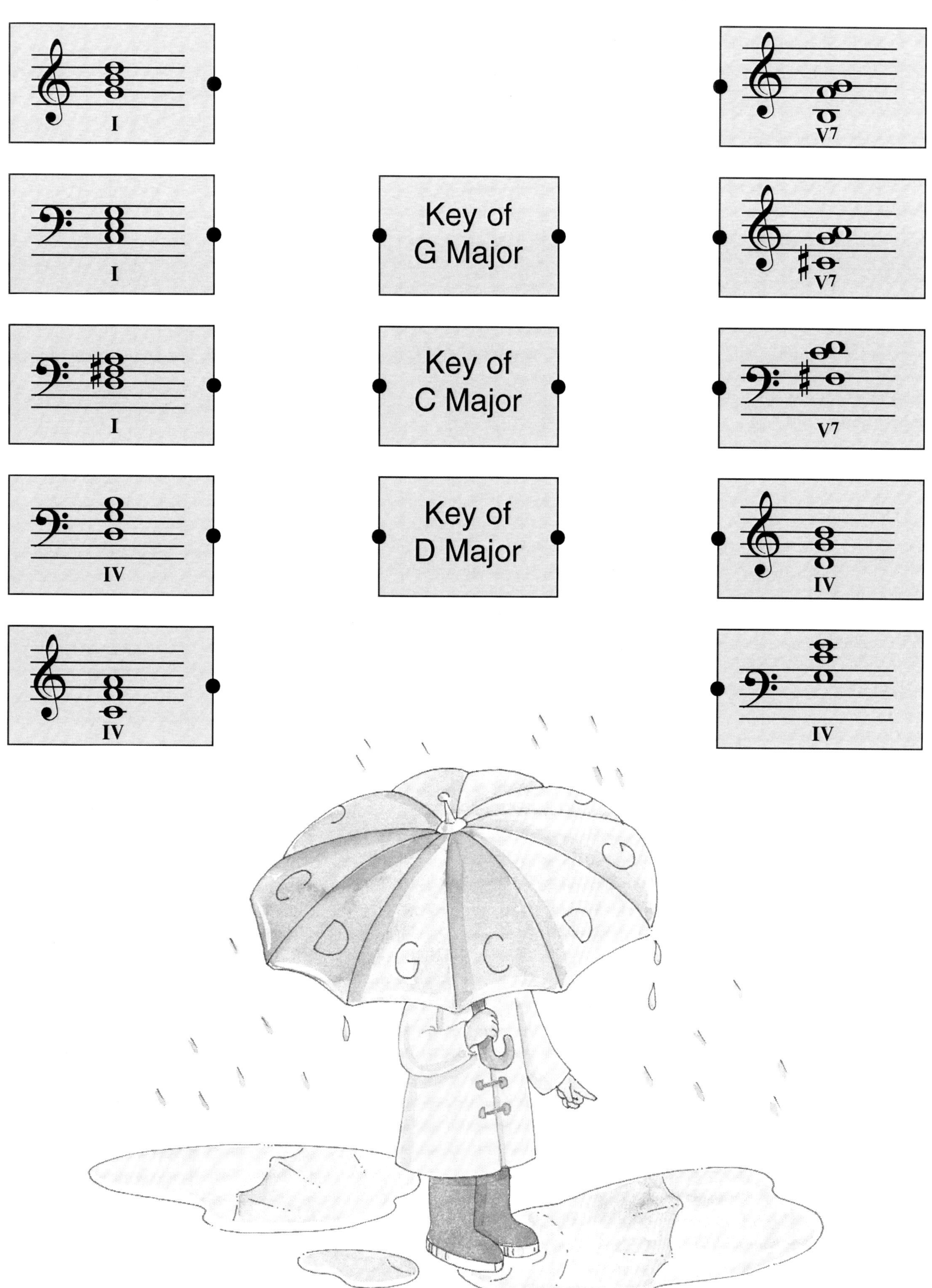

Just Walkin' in the Rain

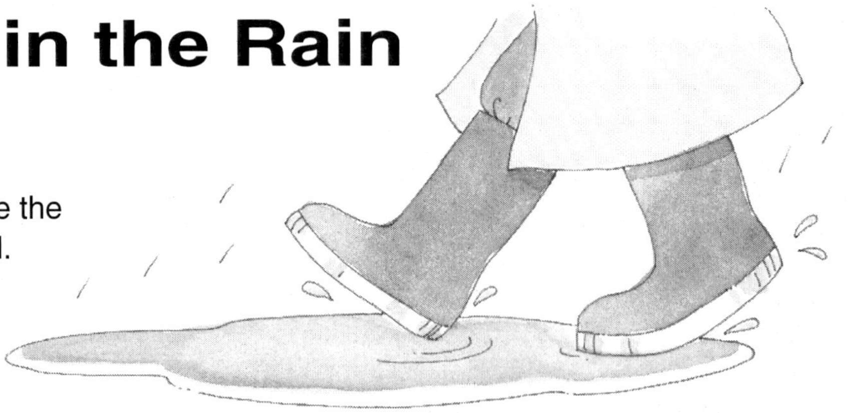

On each line below the chords in *JUST WALKIN' IN THE RAIN,* write the Roman numeral name of the chord.

KEY OF D

Andante moderato

Martha Mier

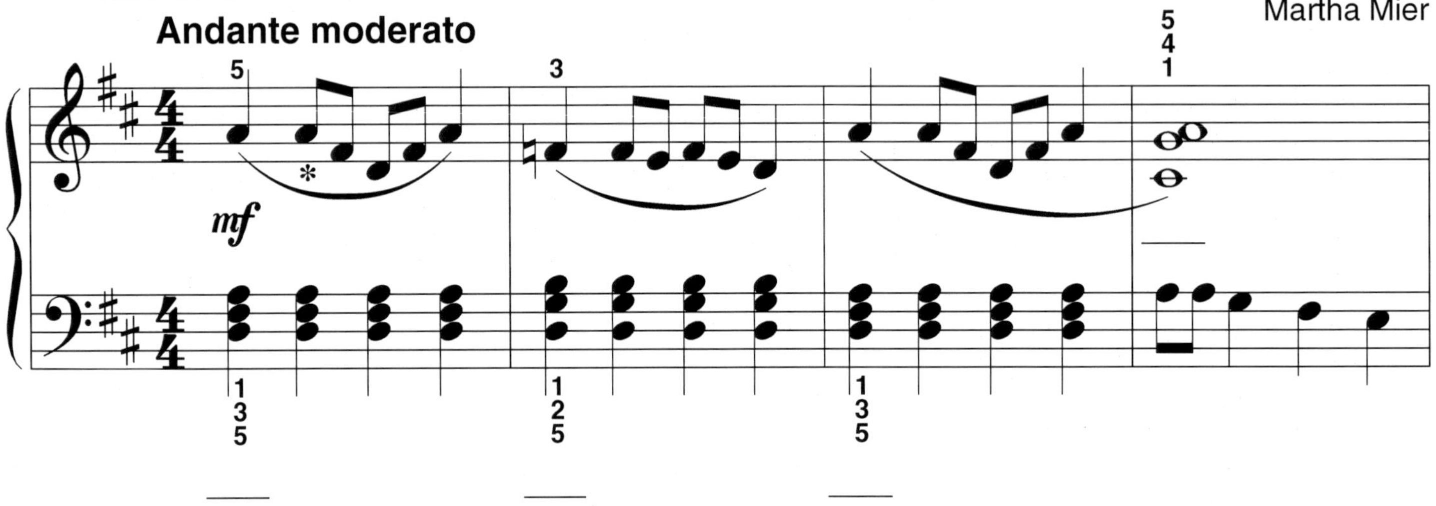

mf

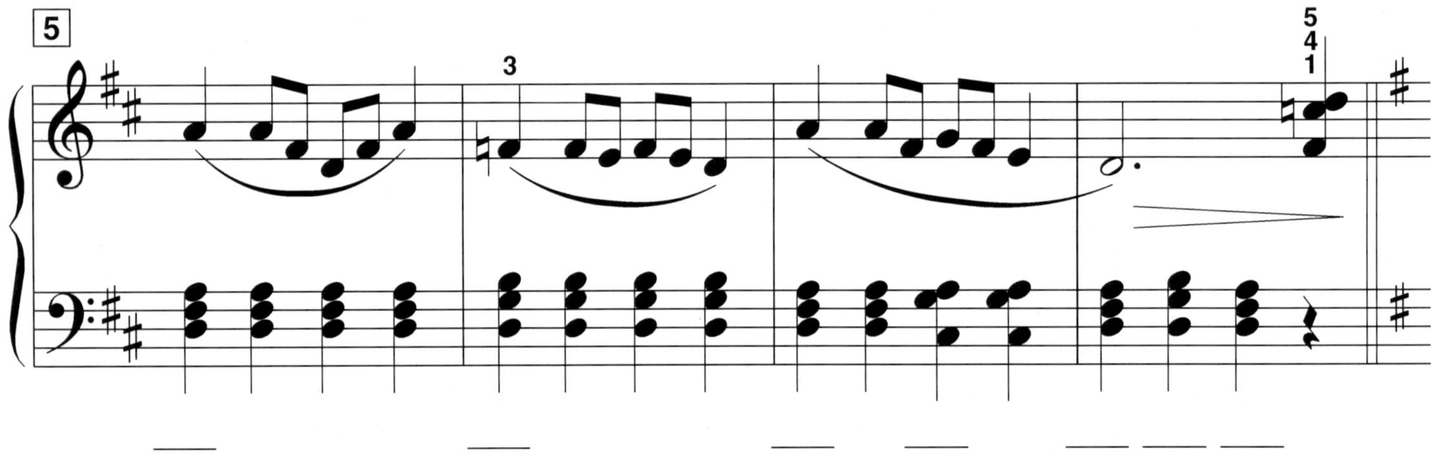

5

KEY OF G

9

mp

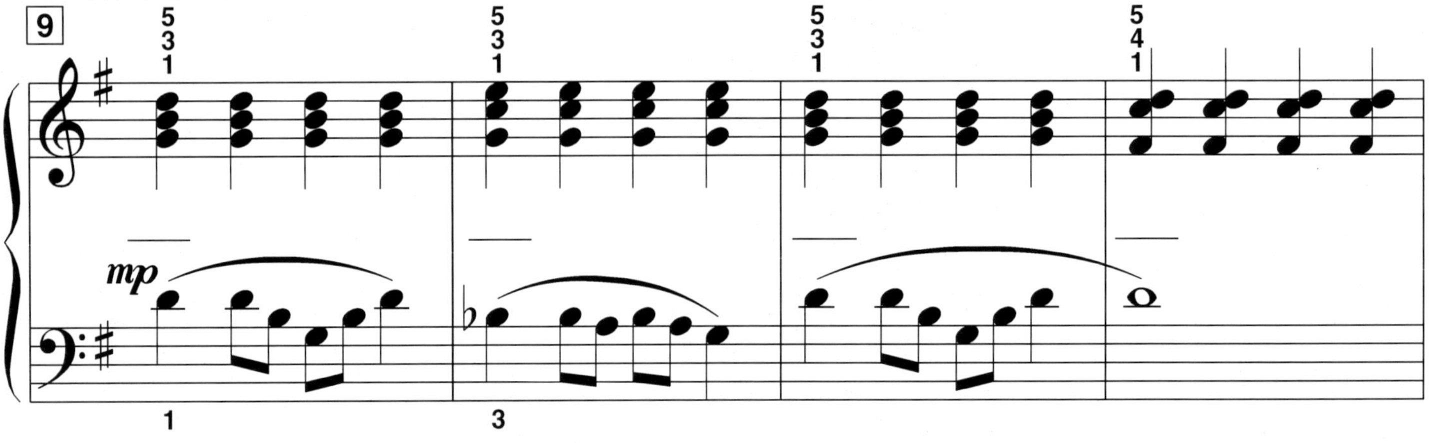

✱ Play pairs of eighth notes unevenly, in a lilting style:

13
3
1
17
KEY OF C
5
3
5
4
1
mf
1
3
5
1
2
5
1
3
5
21
3
25
rit.
mp
5-1
5

Unit 3

Use after page 19.

The Chromatic Scale

The CHROMATIC SCALE goes up and down using only half steps. Every key (both black and white) is played, and no keys are skipped.

The 3rd finger plays each black key. Finger 1 is used on all white keys EXCEPT when two white keys are together, then use 1-2, or 2-1.

Finish writing the LEFT HAND fingering descending (going down):

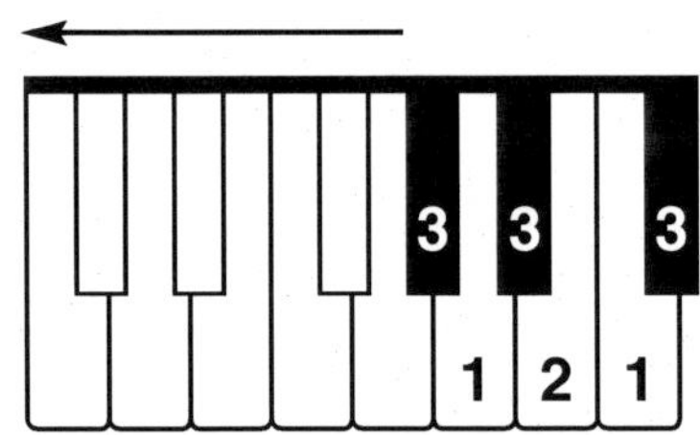

Finish writing the RIGHT HAND fingering ascending (going up):

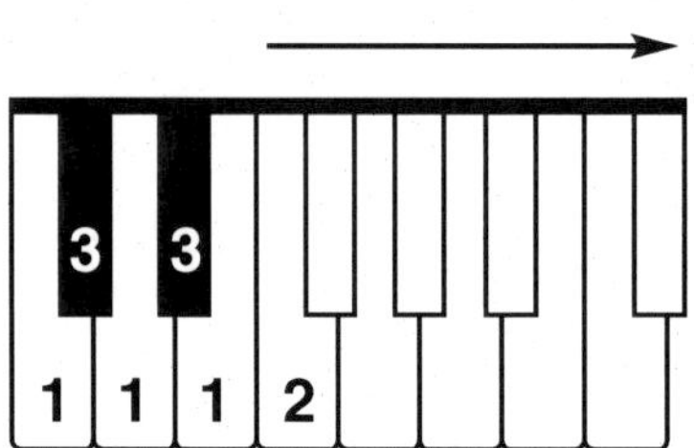

Finish writing the letter names of the CHROMATIC SCALE.

Use sharp names for the black keys when ascending.

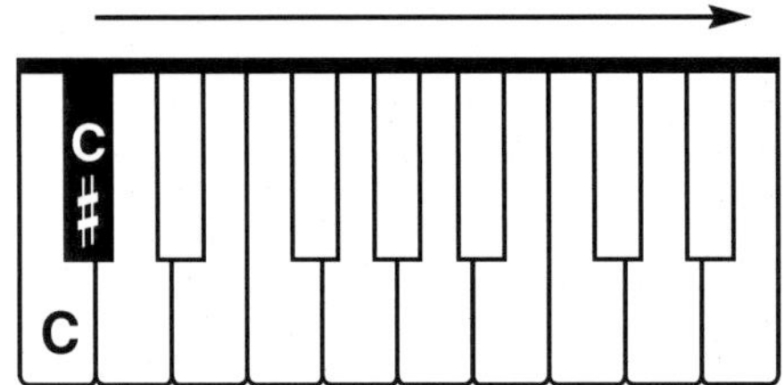

Use flat names for the black keys when descending.

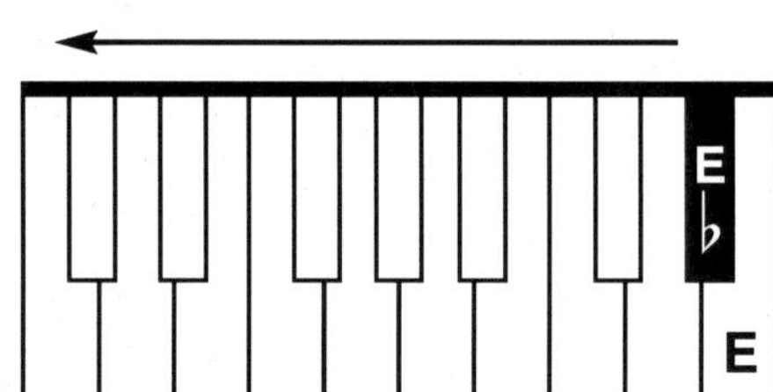

Write the notes of the CHROMATIC SCALE ascending. Use sharp signs for black keys.
Write the finger number over each note. Write the letter name on the line.

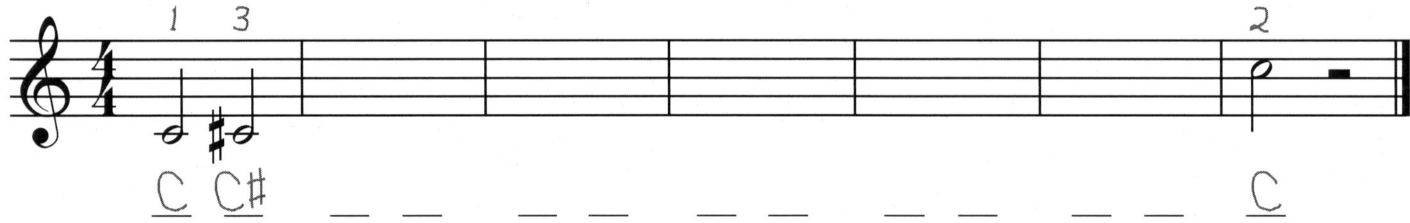

Write the notes of the CHROMATIC SCALE descending. Use flat signs for black keys.
Write the finger number over each note. Write the letter name on the line.

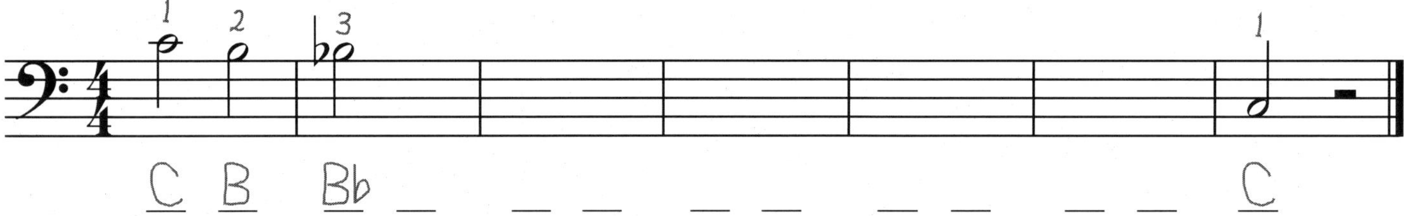

Complete the following sentences, then solve the crossword puzzle.

ACROSS

1. A chromatic scale consists of only ____________ steps.

2. A scale consisting of only half steps is called a ______________________ scale.

3. In a descending (going down) chromatic scale, ____________ are used to name the black keys.

4. In an ascending (going up) chromatic scale, _______________ are used to name the black keys.

5. Finger 1 is used on all ___________________ keys, except when two white keys are together.

DOWN

6. The black keys in the chromatic scale are all played with the _____________ finger.

Practice this WARM-UP before playing *JAZZY HALF STEPS.*

Jazzy Half Steps

Circle each one-octave chromatic scale in *JAZZY HALF STEPS.*

Allegro moderato

Martha Mier

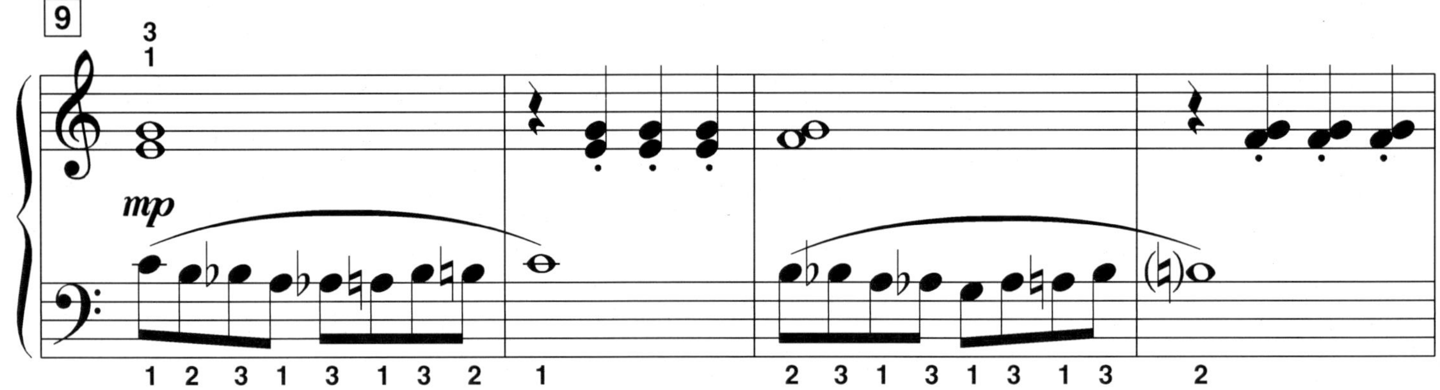

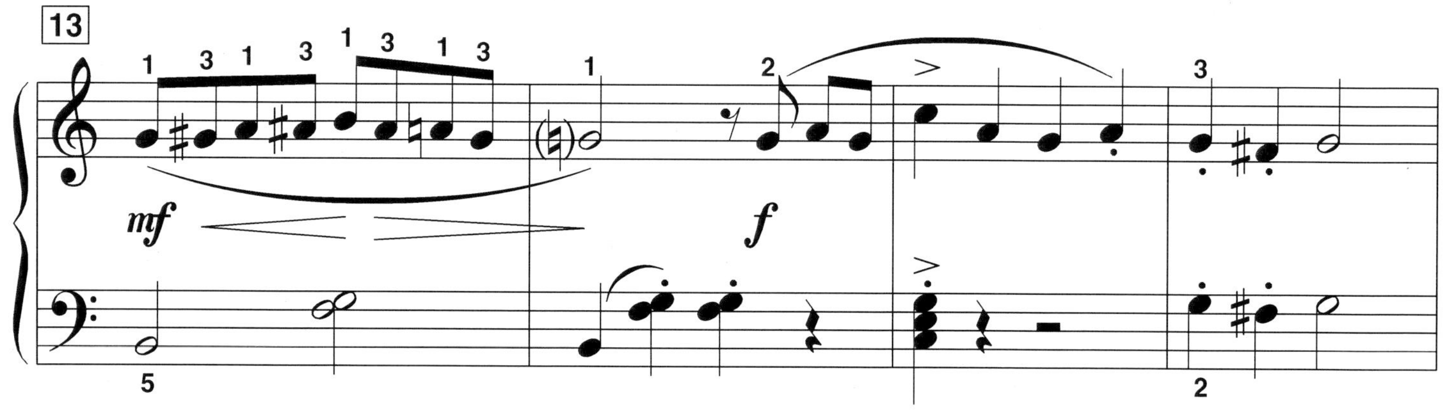
13
mf
f

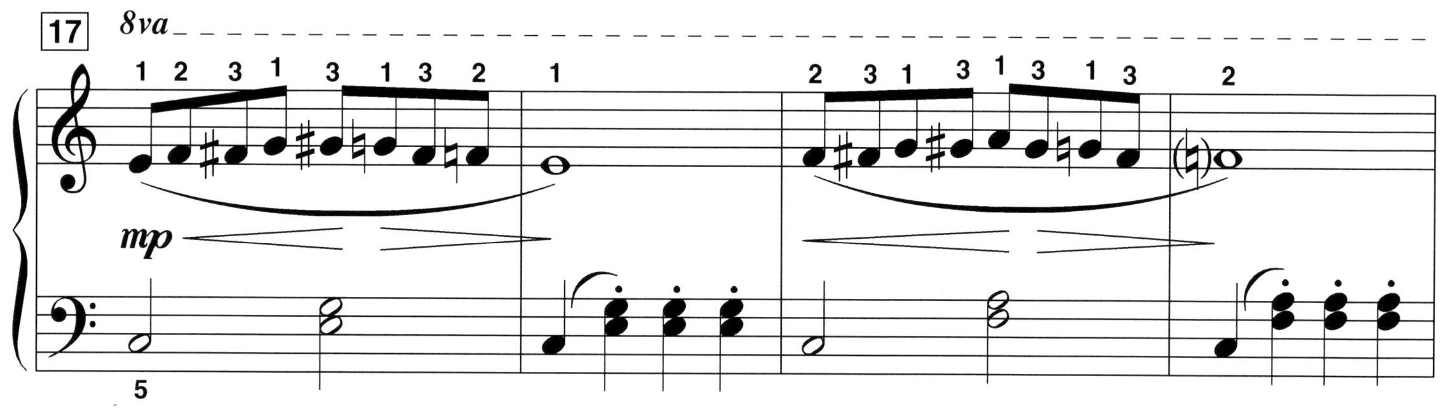
17
8va
mp

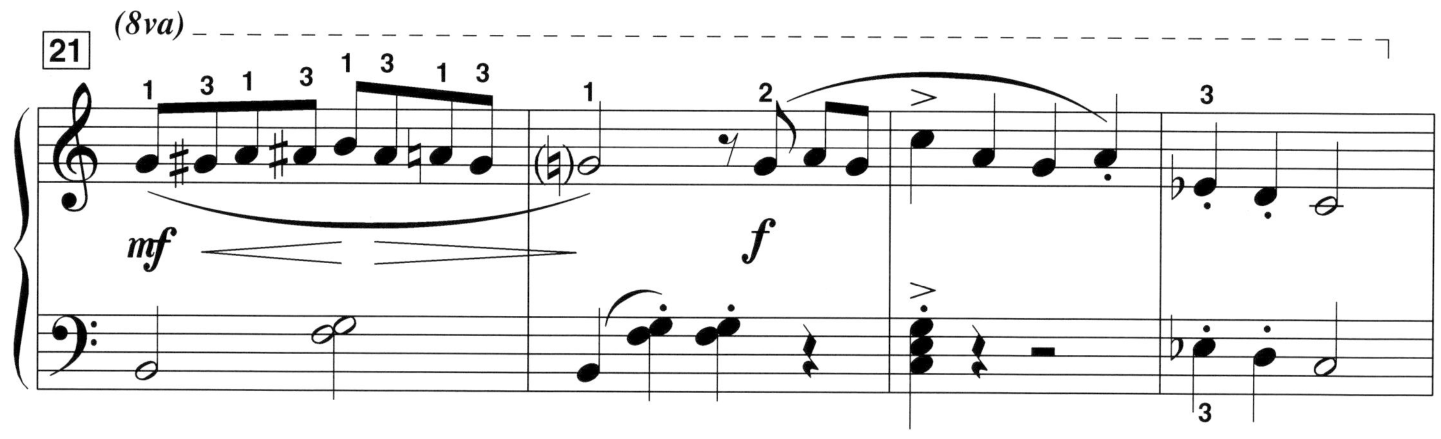
21
(8va)
mf
f

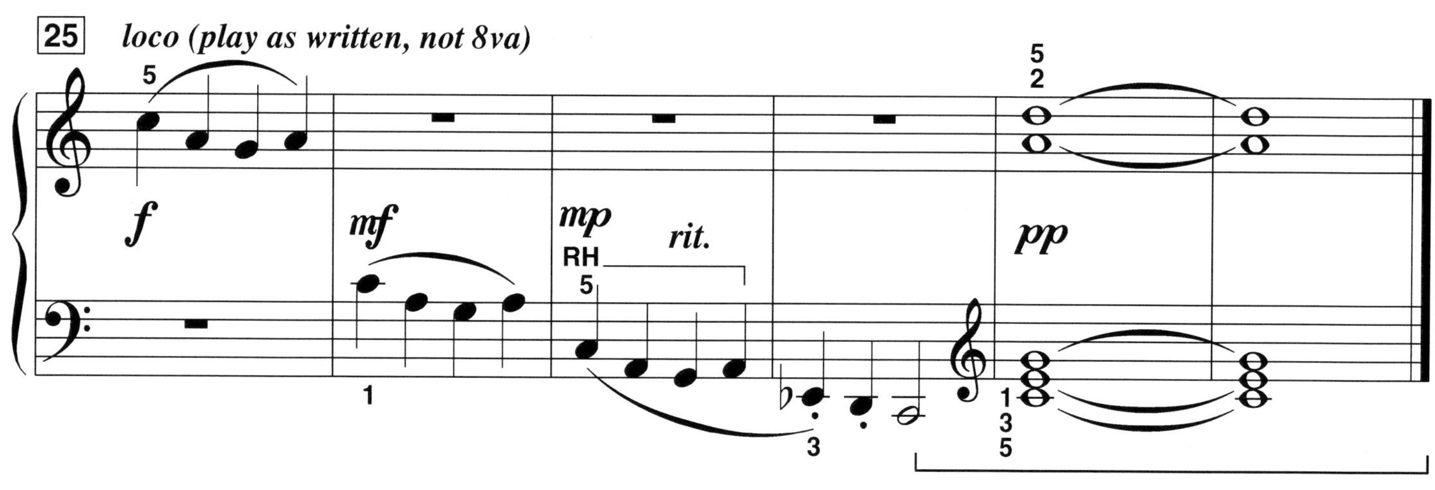
25
loco (play as written, not 8va)
f
mf
mp
rit.
RH
pp

Unit 4

Use after page 21.

The F Major Scale

The MAJOR SCALE is made of two tetrachords joined by a whole step.

The pattern of whole steps and half steps of a major scale is:

WHOLE STEP—WHOLE STEP—HALF STEP / WHOLE STEP / WHOLE STEP—WHOLE STEP—HALF STEP

Using the pattern of whole steps and half steps of the major scale, write the letter names of the F major scale on the keys.

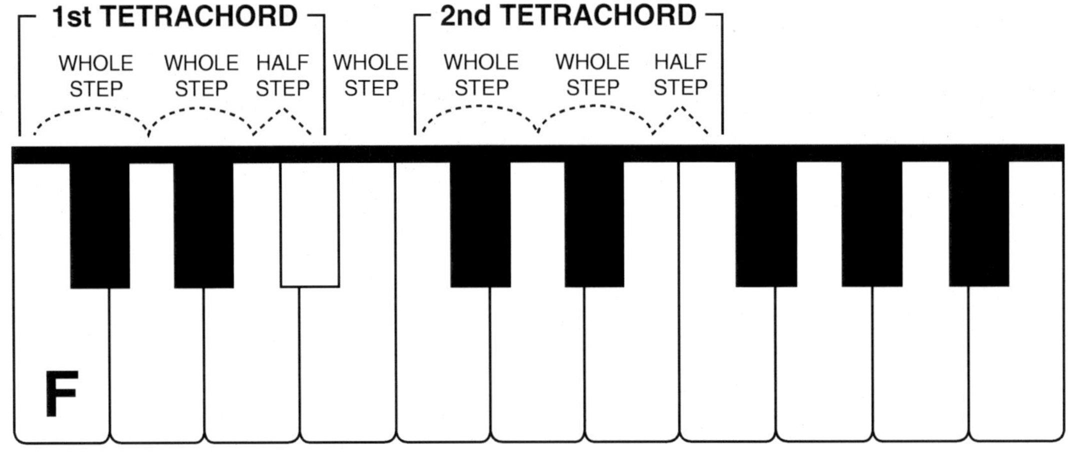

Using the pattern of whole steps and half steps of the major scale, write the notes of the F major scale on the staff in both treble and bass clef. Use whole notes.

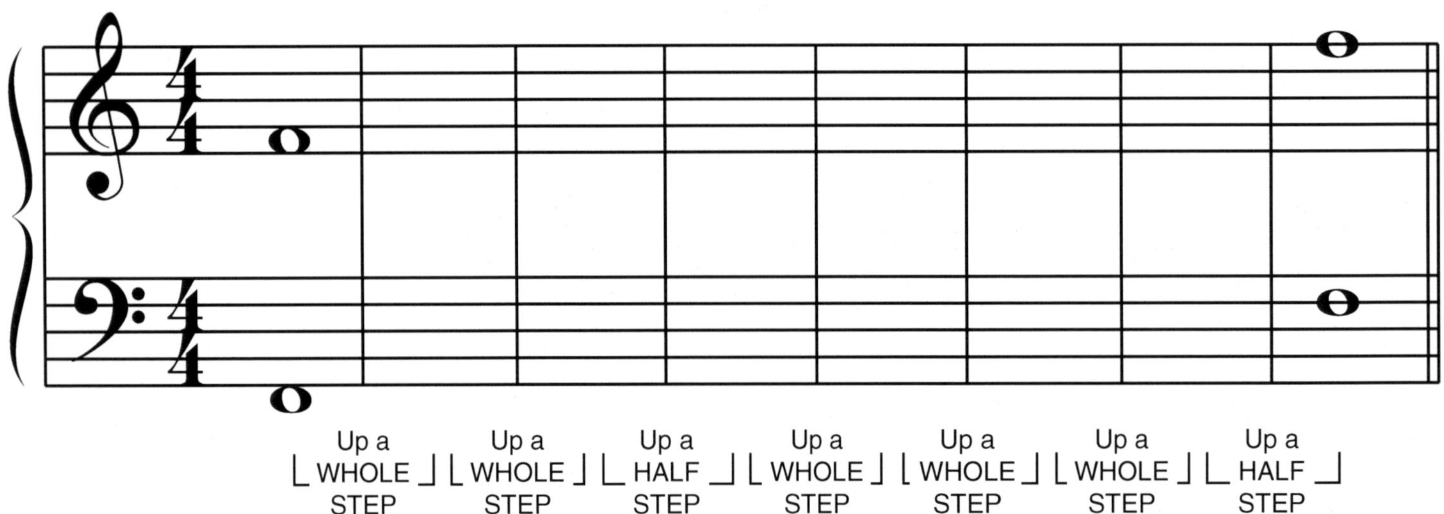

Circle the number of sharps or flats found in the key of F MAJOR.

TWO FLATS   ONE FLAT   ONE SHARP

Circle the F MAJOR key signature.

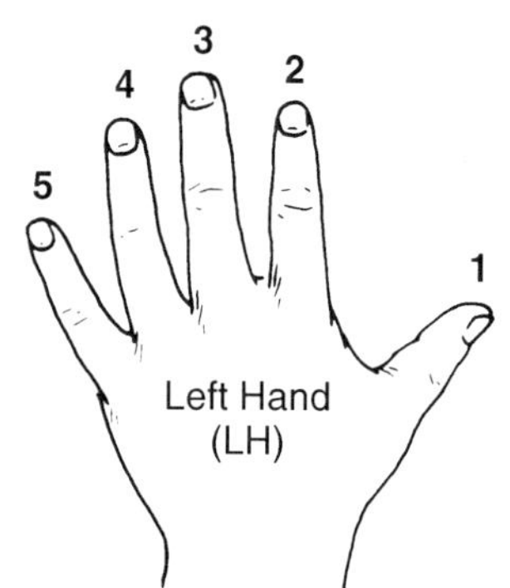

F Scale Fingering

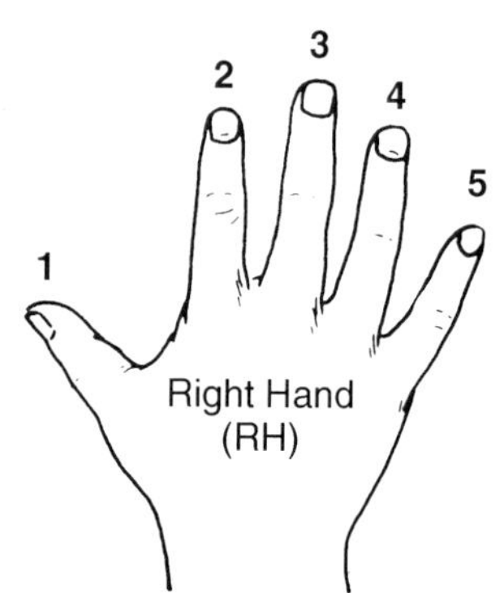

In the boxes below the keys, write the finger numbers for playing the scale.

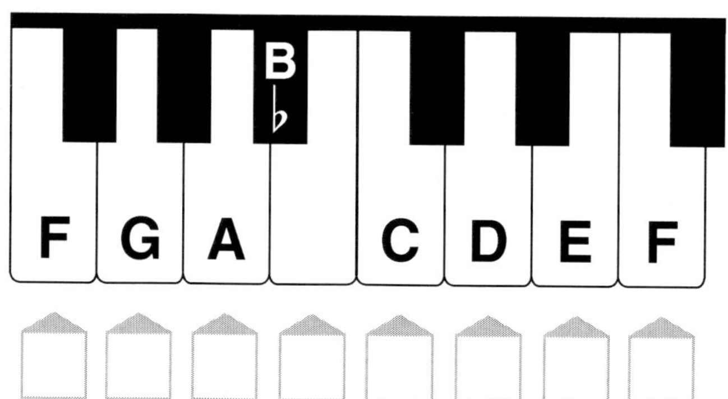

RIGHT HAND

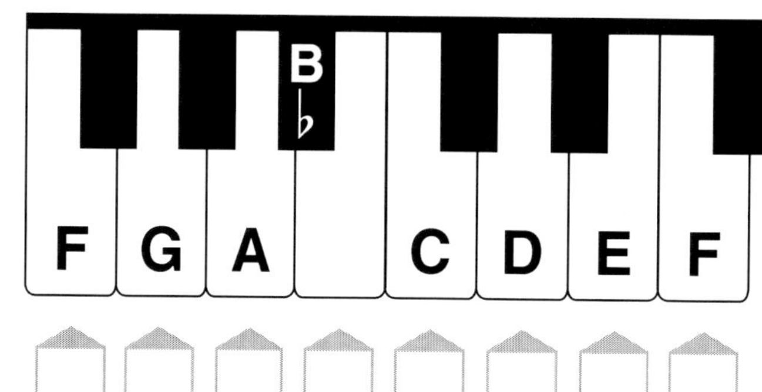

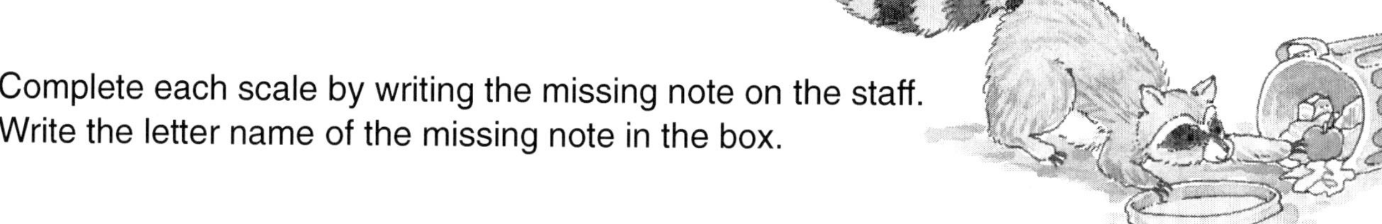

Complete each scale by writing the missing note on the staff.
Write the letter name of the missing note in the box.

1.
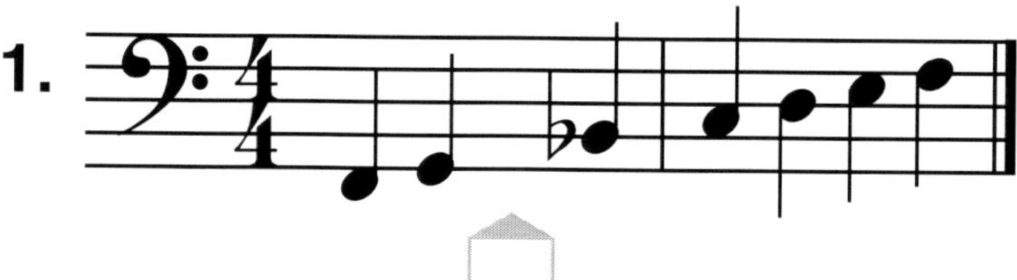

3.

2.
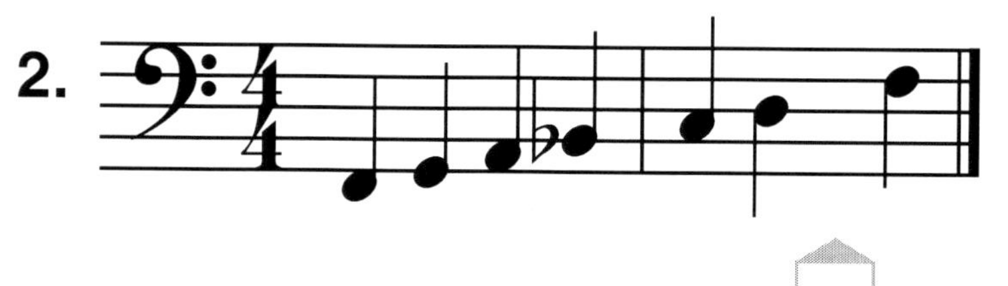

4.
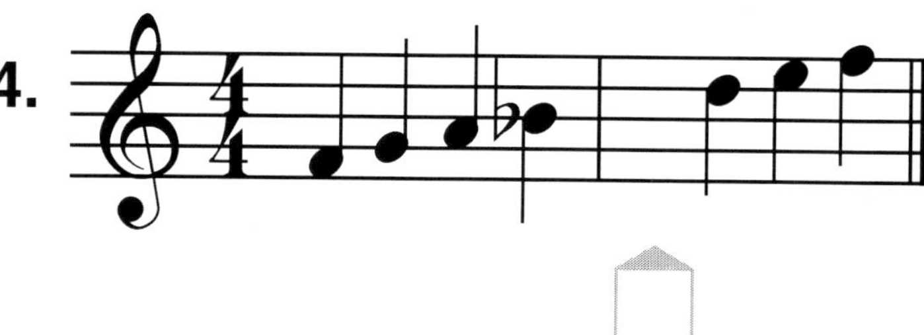

Complete the mystery sentence using the names of the missing notes from the above exercise.
Use the missing note in No. 1 above for blank 1 in the sentence, etc.

"You __r__ top o__ th__ __l__ss!"

1. 2. 3. 2. 4. 1.

Raccoon Ramble

Circle each F major scale in *RACCOON RAMBLE.*

Martha Mier

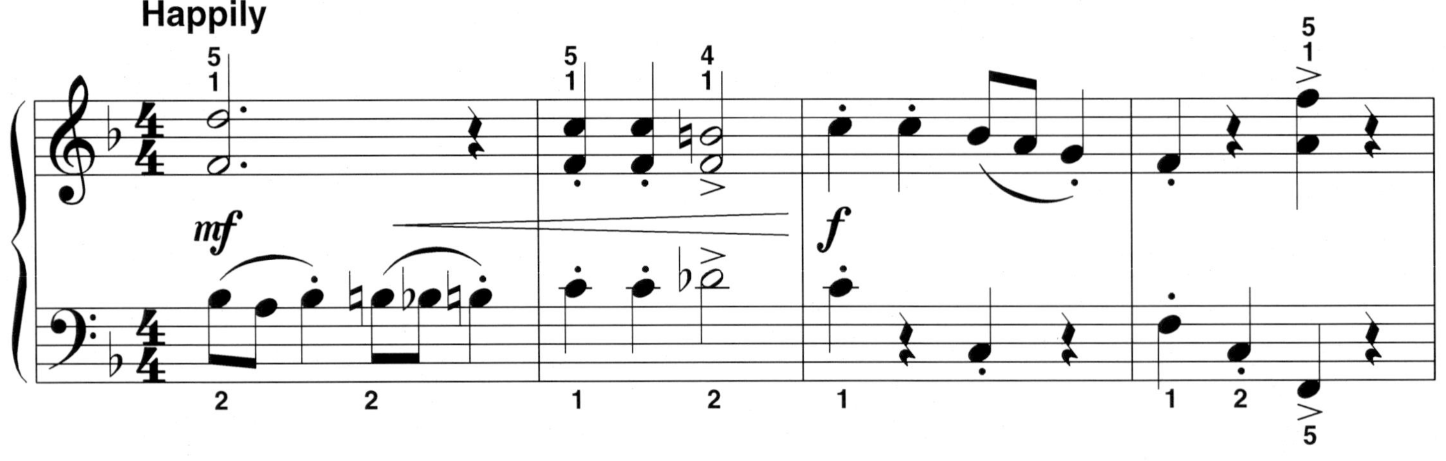

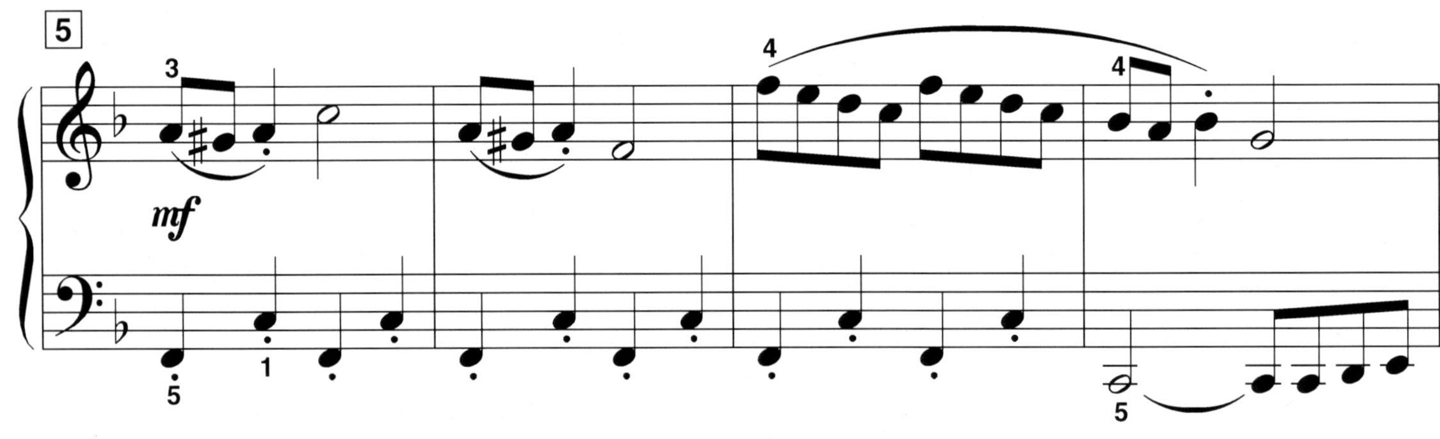

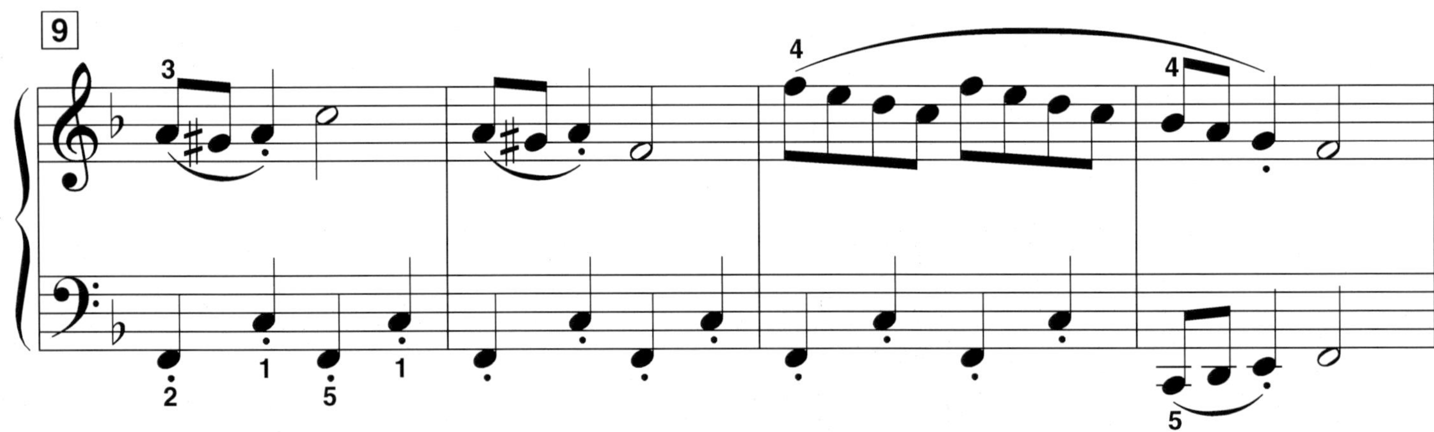

17
mp
f
21
mf
25
29
p
f
ff
8va

Use after page 23.

Unit 5

Primary Triads—Key of F Major

The PRIMARY TRIADS of any key are built on the 1st, 4th and 5th notes of the scale.

Primary Triads in the Key of F Major

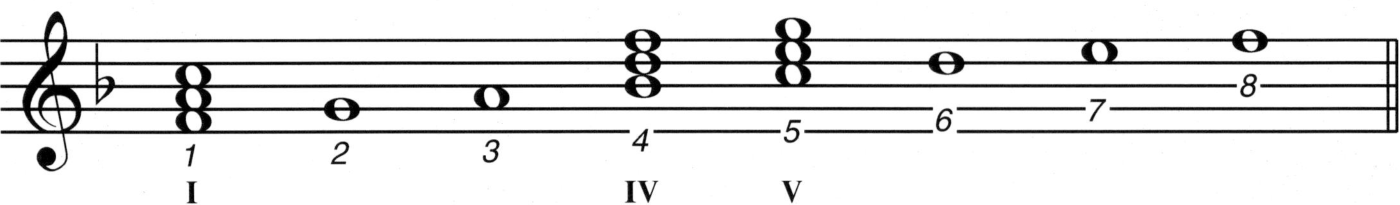

In the KEY OF F MAJOR, the PRIMARY TRIADS are built on the notes: _____ (I) _____ (IV) and _____ (V) .

On the keyboards below, write the letter names for the notes of the primary triads in the key of F major.

I Chord

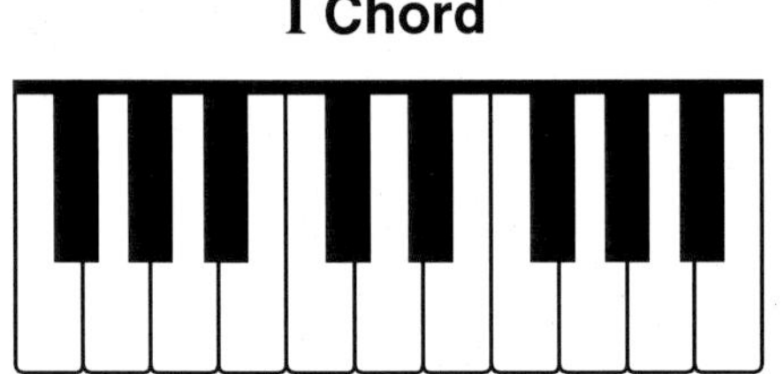

IV Chord

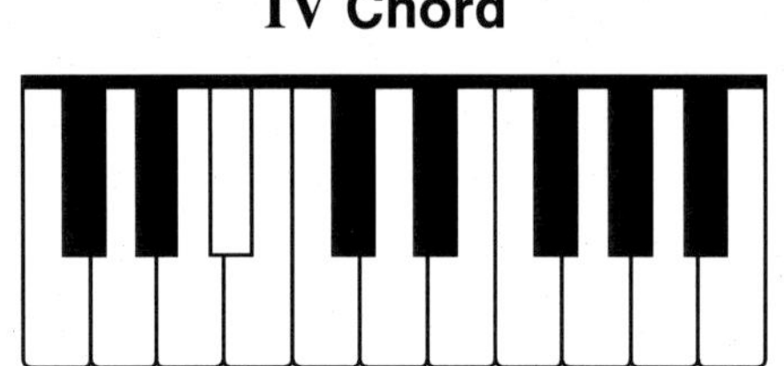

V Chord

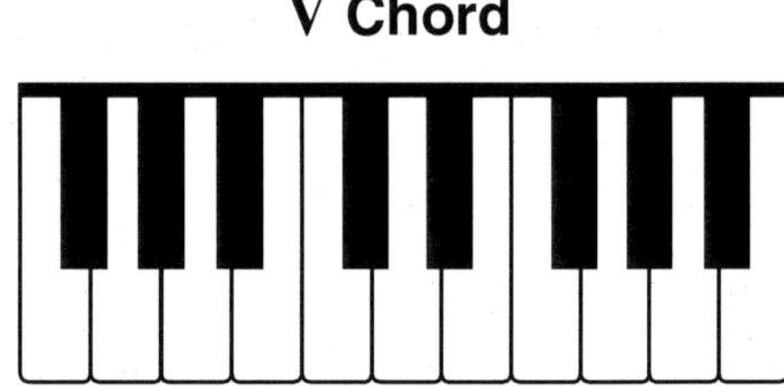

In the boxes above the triads, write the letter names of the notes of the triad.
On the top line below the staff, write the Roman numeral name of the triad in the key of F major.
On the bottom line, write the letter name of the chord.

Letter Names: C / A / F

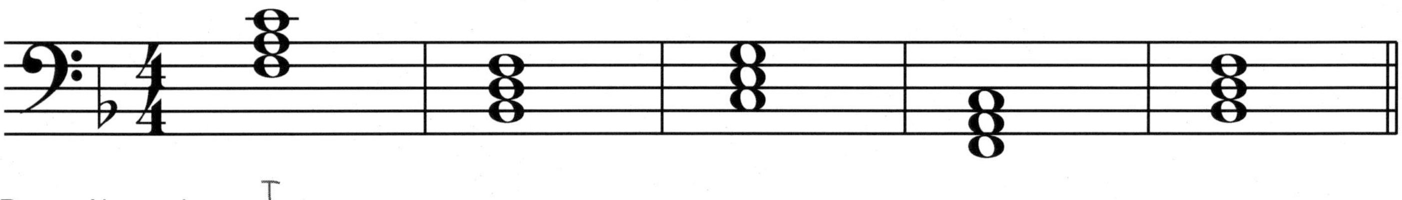

Roman Numeral: I

Chord Name: F

F Major Chord Progression

Primary Chords

To make playing the **I**, **IV** and **V** (or V^7) chords smoother moving from one to the other, the notes may be rearranged. The same notes must be used, but they may be played in different octaves.

IN ROOT POSITION | **SMOOTHER CHORD PROGRESSION**

The **I** chord (F chord) stays the same.

The top note (F) of the **IV** chord (B♭ chord) is moved down an octave.

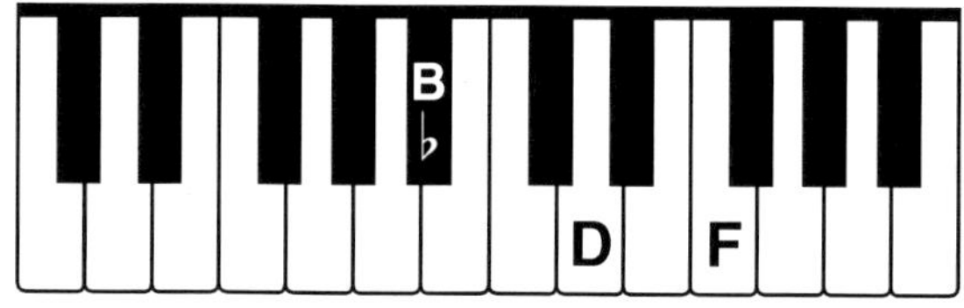

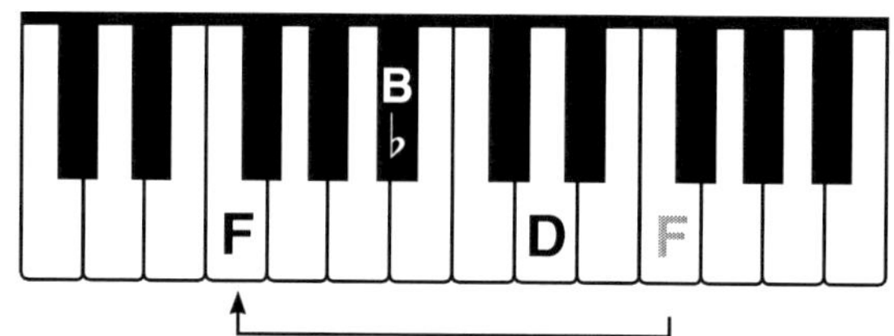

To make the V^7 chord (C^7 chord), first add the 7th tone (B♭) to the **V** chord (C chord). Move the root (C) up an octave, and leave out the 5th (G).

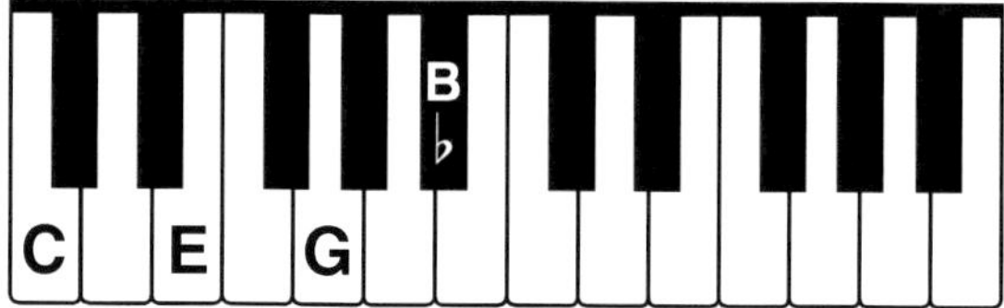

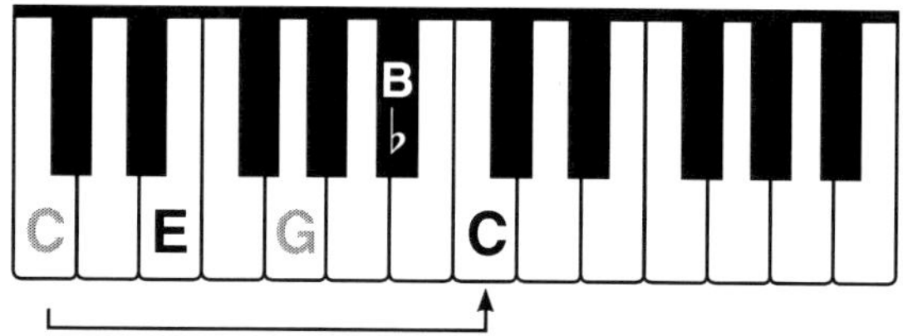

Play these examples of root position chords and the smoother chord progression.

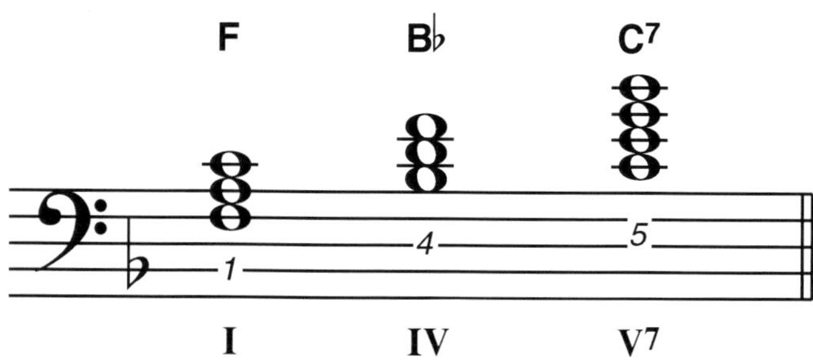

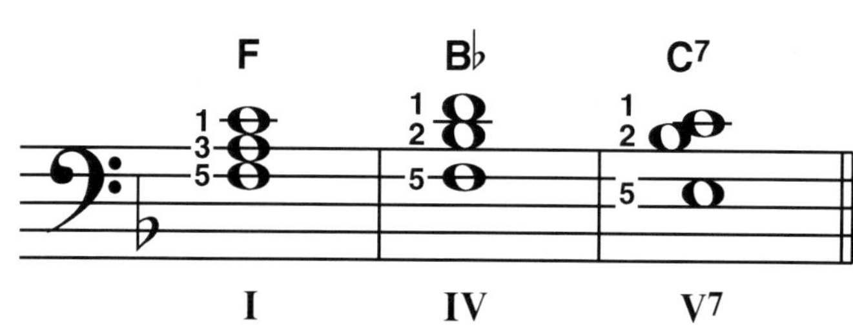

Write the correct Roman numeral on the line below the following chords from the key of F.

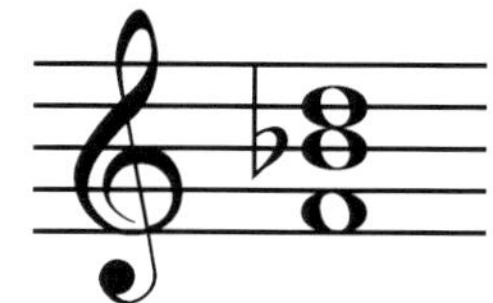

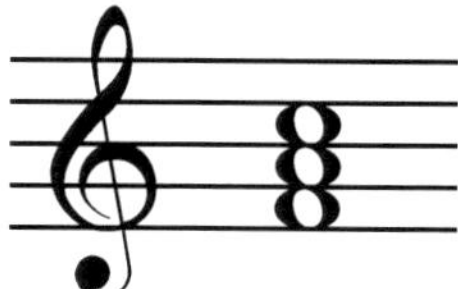

A Little Bit Country

On each line below the left-hand broken chords in *A LITTLE BIT COUNTRY,* write the Roman numeral name of the chord.

Slow waltz tempo

Martha Mier

mf

5 5 2 1 2

5 1 3 5 1 2

____ ____ ____ ____

5

3

5 1 2 5 1 2 5

____ ____

9

5 1 1

5

____ ____ ____ ____

13

5

f

5 2-1 2 5

____

17
5
2
5
2
5

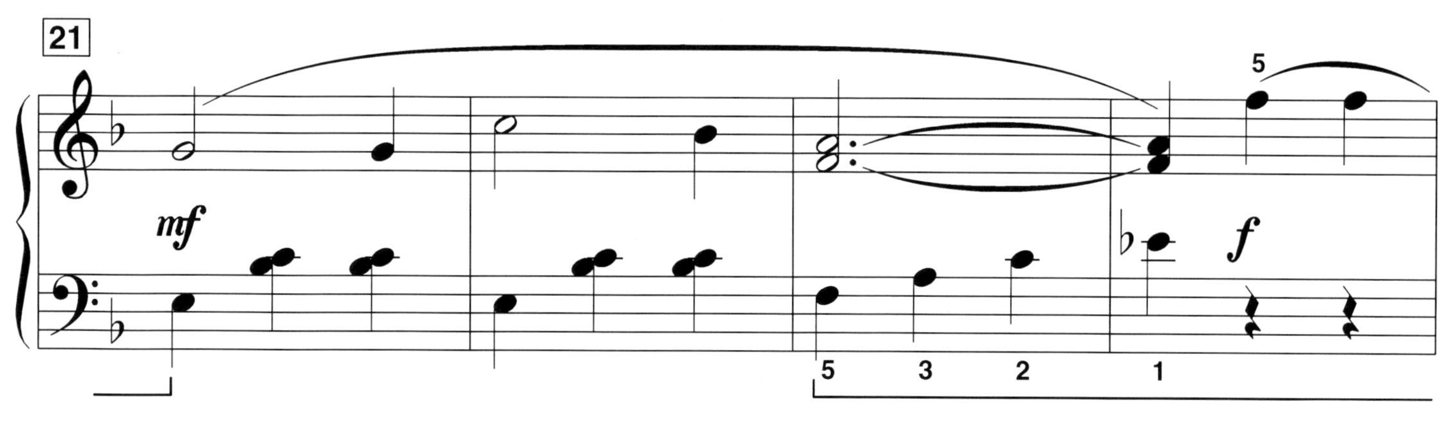
21
5
mf
f
5
3
2
1

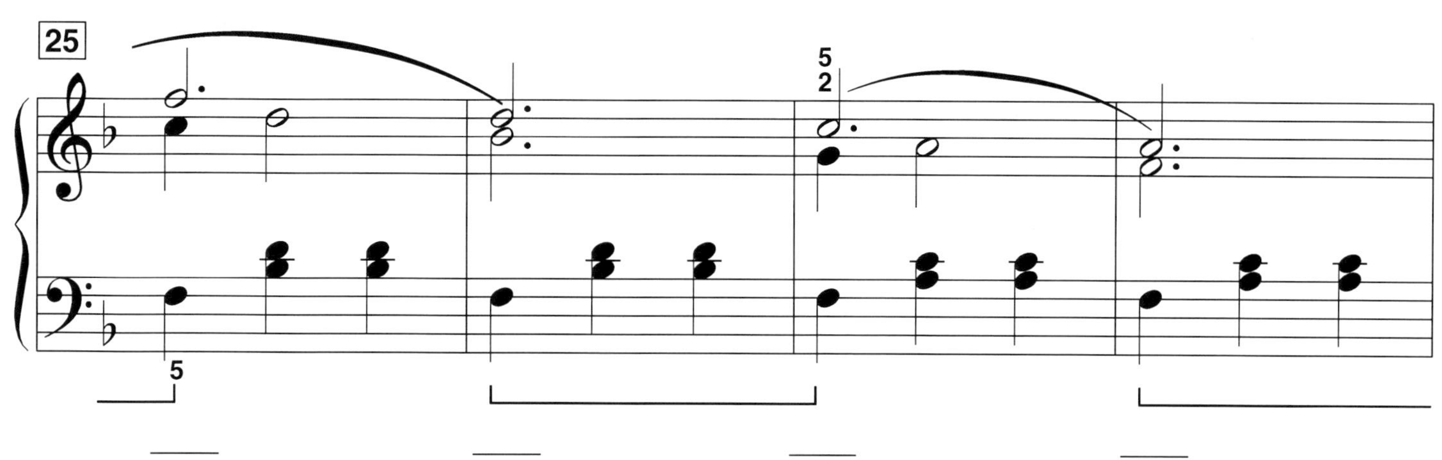
25
5
2
5

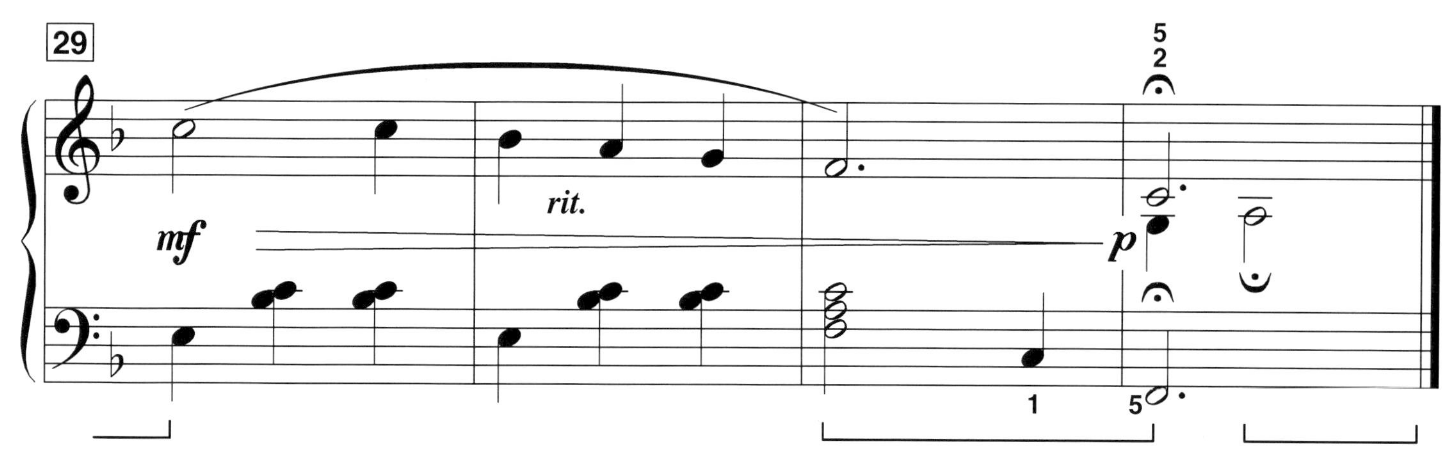
29
5
2
mf
rit.
p
1
5

Unit 6

Use after page 25.

The Key of A Minor
(Relative of C Major)

Each major key has a RELATIVE MINOR key. It is called "relative" because it has the same key signature as the major key.

HOW TO FIND THE RELATIVE MINOR SCALE
The relative minor scale begins on the *6th tone* of the major scale, for example:

C MAJOR SCALE

A MINOR SCALE

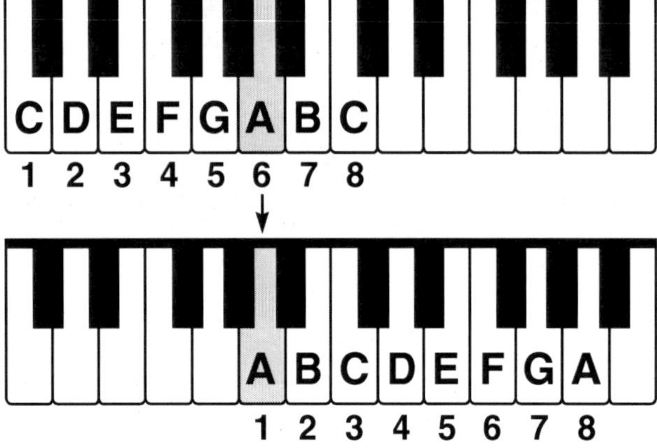

THE THREE KINDS OF MINOR SCALES

1. The NATURAL MINOR SCALE
   This scale uses the tones of the relative major scale.

2. The HARMONIC MINOR SCALE
   The 7th tone (G) is raised one half step, ascending and descending.

3. The MELODIC MINOR SCALE
   In the *ascending* scale, the 6th (F) and 7th (G) tones are raised one half step.

The *descending* scale is the same as the natural minor.

Ascending ⟶

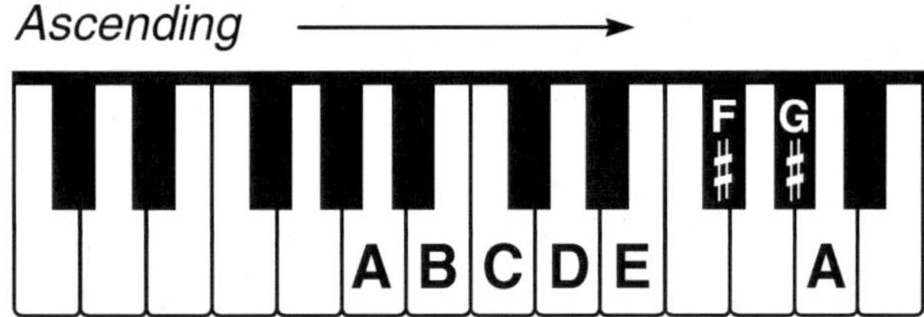

⟵ *Descending*

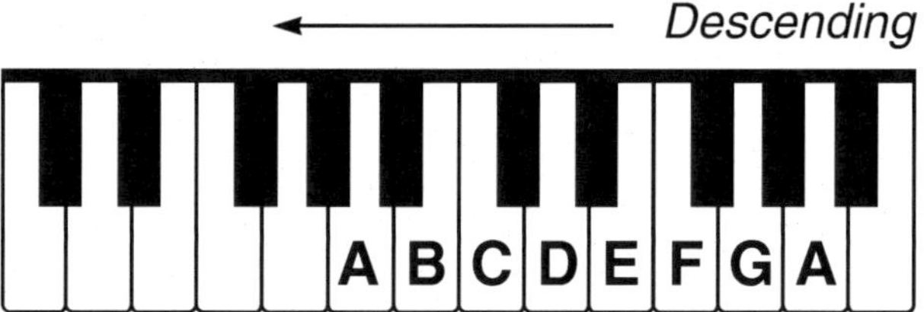

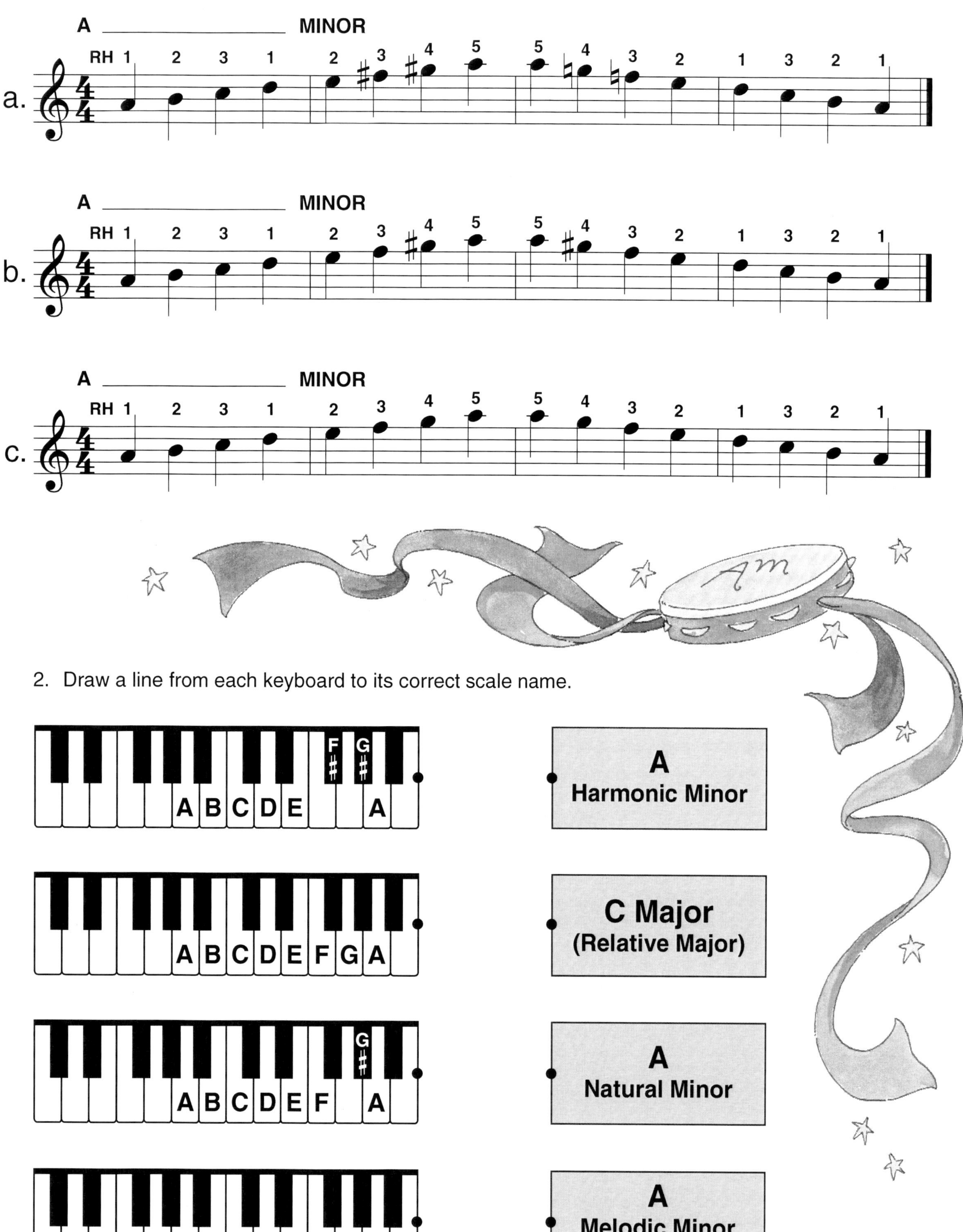
1. Play the following scales. Fill in the name of each scale (natural, harmonic or melodic).
a.
A ________________ MINOR
RH 1 2 3 1 2 3 4 5 5 4 3 2 1 3 2 1
b.
A ________________ MINOR
RH 1 2 3 1 2 3 4 5 5 4 3 2 1 3 2 1
c.
A ________________ MINOR
RH 1 2 3 1 2 3 4 5 5 4 3 2 1 3 2 1
Am
2. Draw a line from each keyboard to its correct scale name.
F♯ G♯
A B C D E A
A B C D E F G A
G♯
A B C D E F A
C D E F G A B C
A
Harmonic Minor
C Major
(Relative Major)
A
Natural Minor
A
Melodic Minor
(ascending)

Gypsy Dancers

Circle each A minor scale in *GYPSY DANCERS.*

Lively

Martha Mier

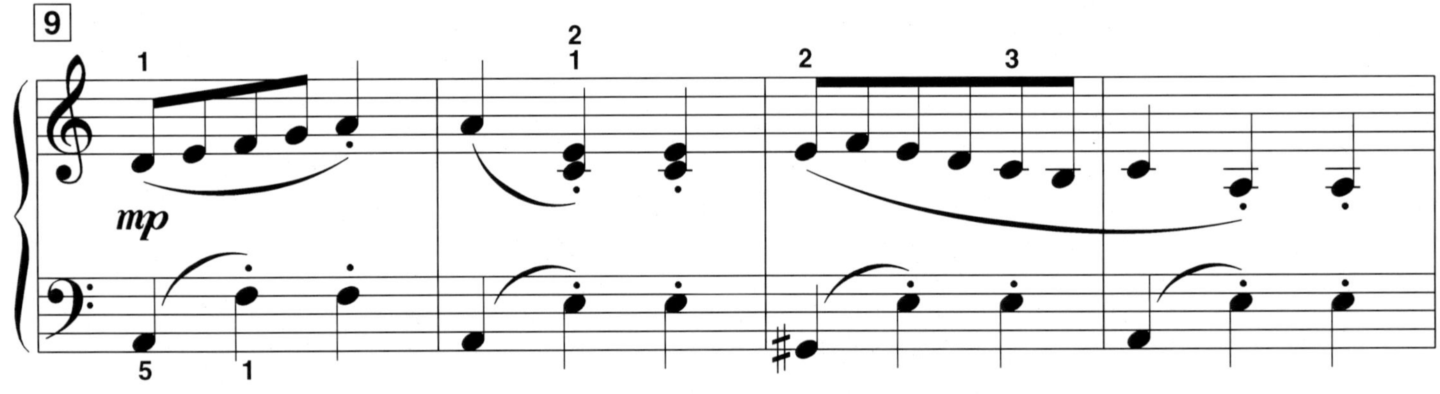

17
1
1
1
3

21
1
3

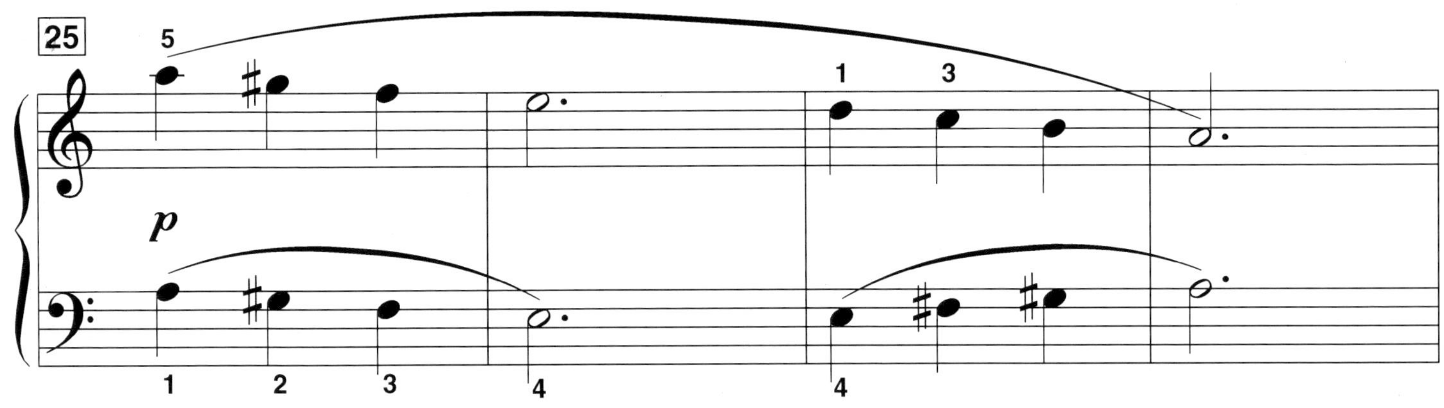
25
5
1
3
p
1
2
3
4
4

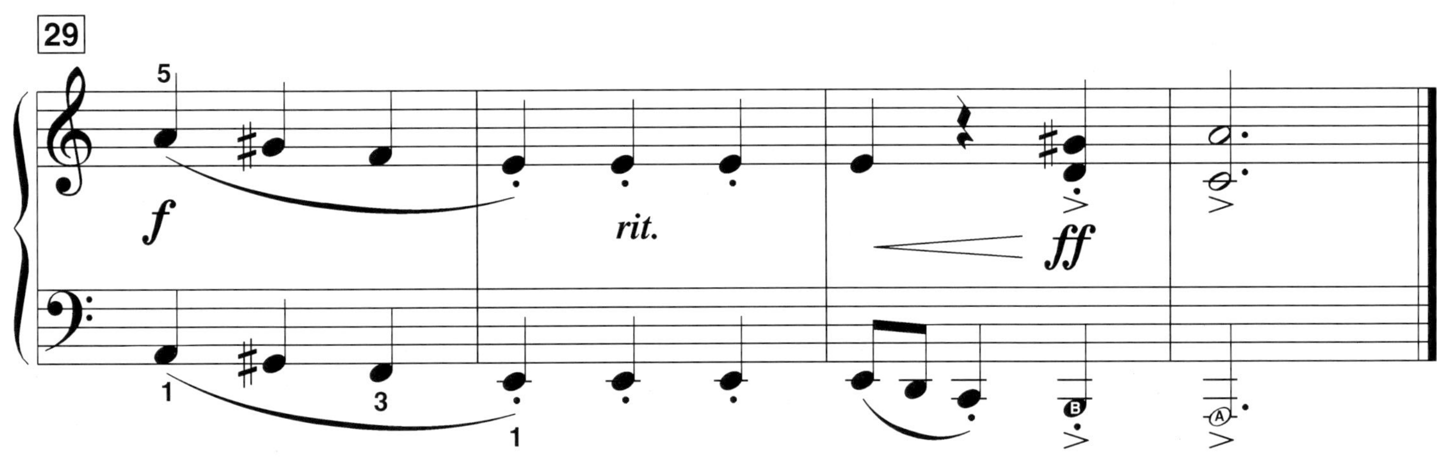
29
5
f
rit.
ff
1
3
1
B
A

Unit 7

Use after page 33.

Major Triads & Minor Triads

MAJOR TRIADS consist of a ROOT, **MAJOR** 3rd and PERFECT 5th.

MINOR TRIADS consist of a ROOT, **MINOR** 3rd and PERFECT 5th.

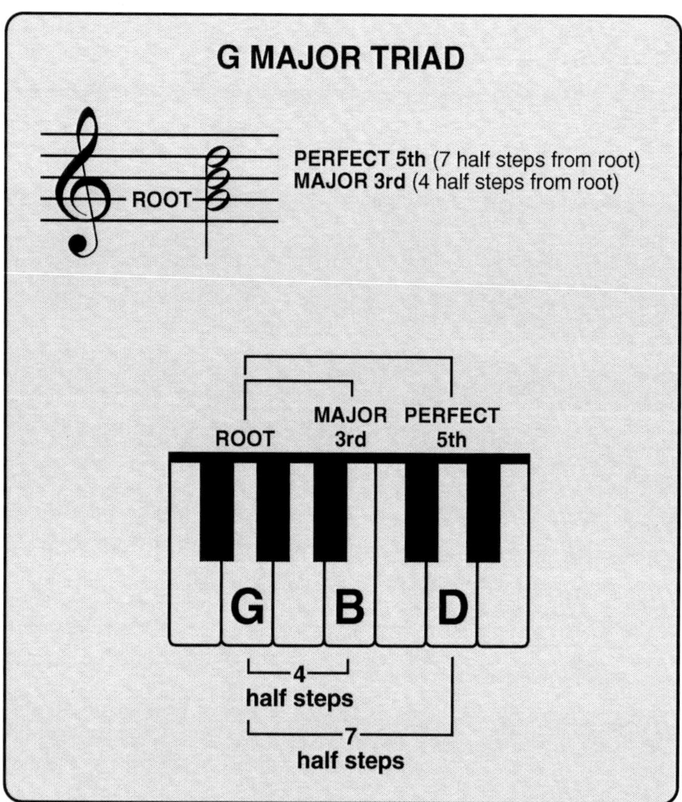

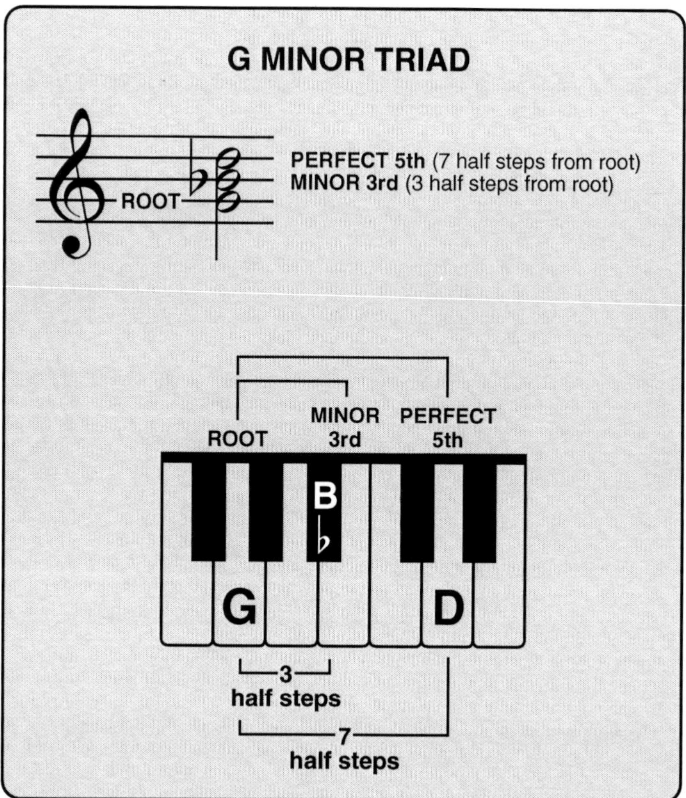

On the line under each keyboard, write M3 for each major 3rd (4 half steps) or m3 for each minor 3rd (3 half steps).

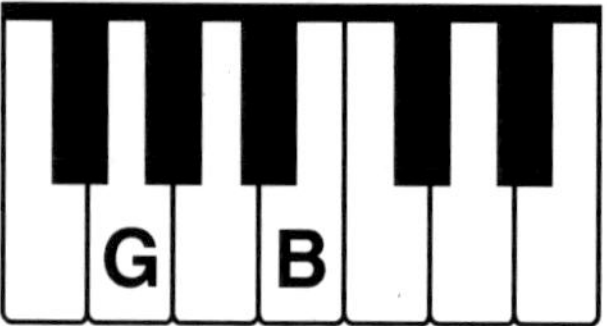

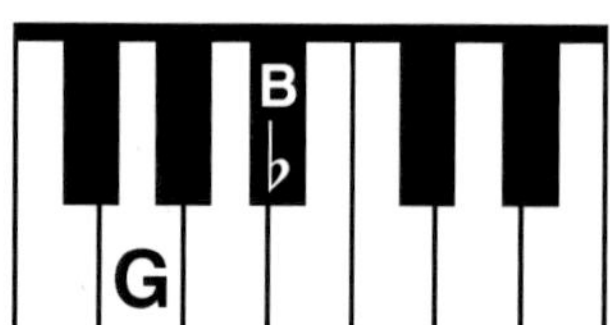

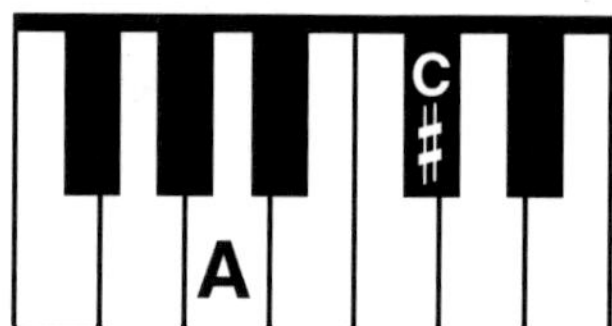

Write the letter name on the key that is a perfect 5th (7 half steps) above the given note.

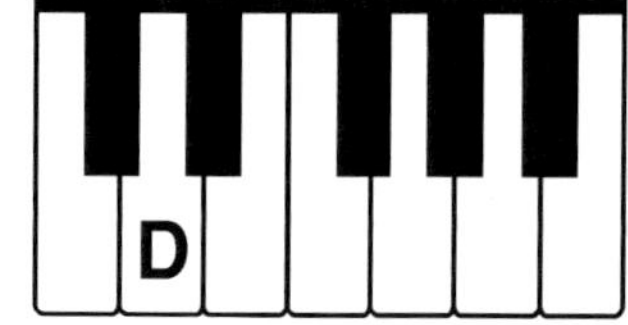

Write letter names on the keys to build each triad.

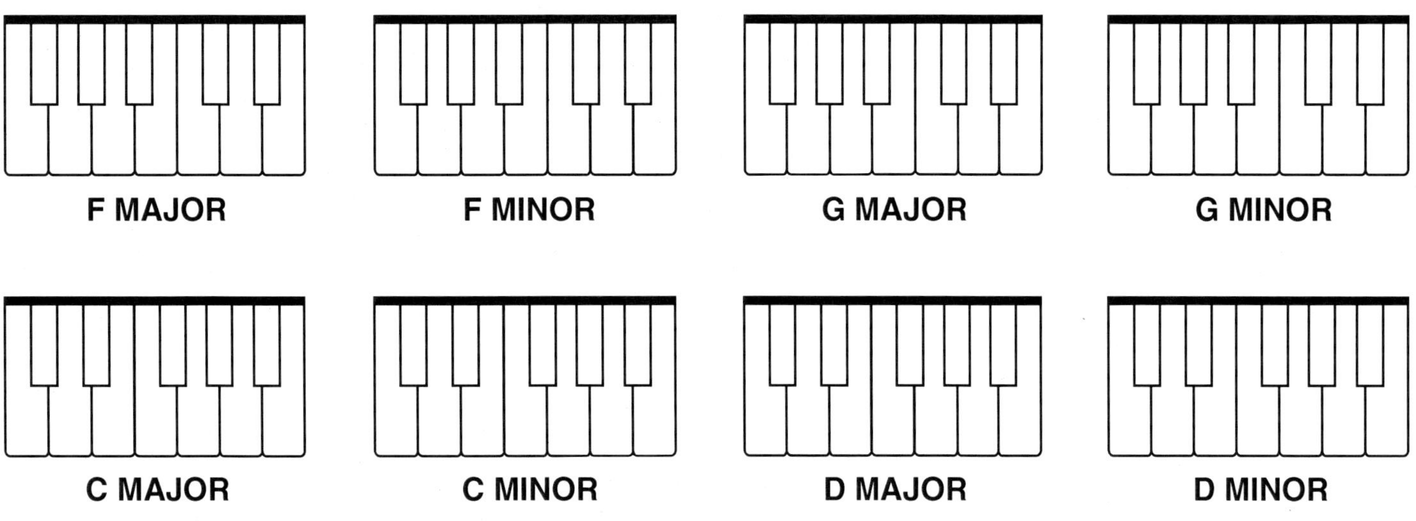

Write whole notes on the staff to build each triad.

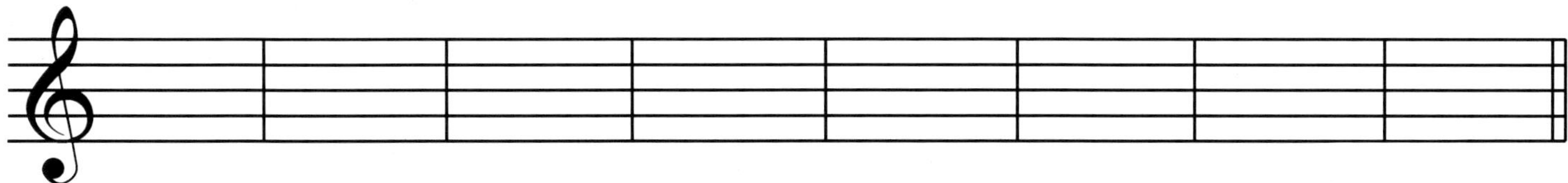

Match each chord name to the correct keyboard and staff.

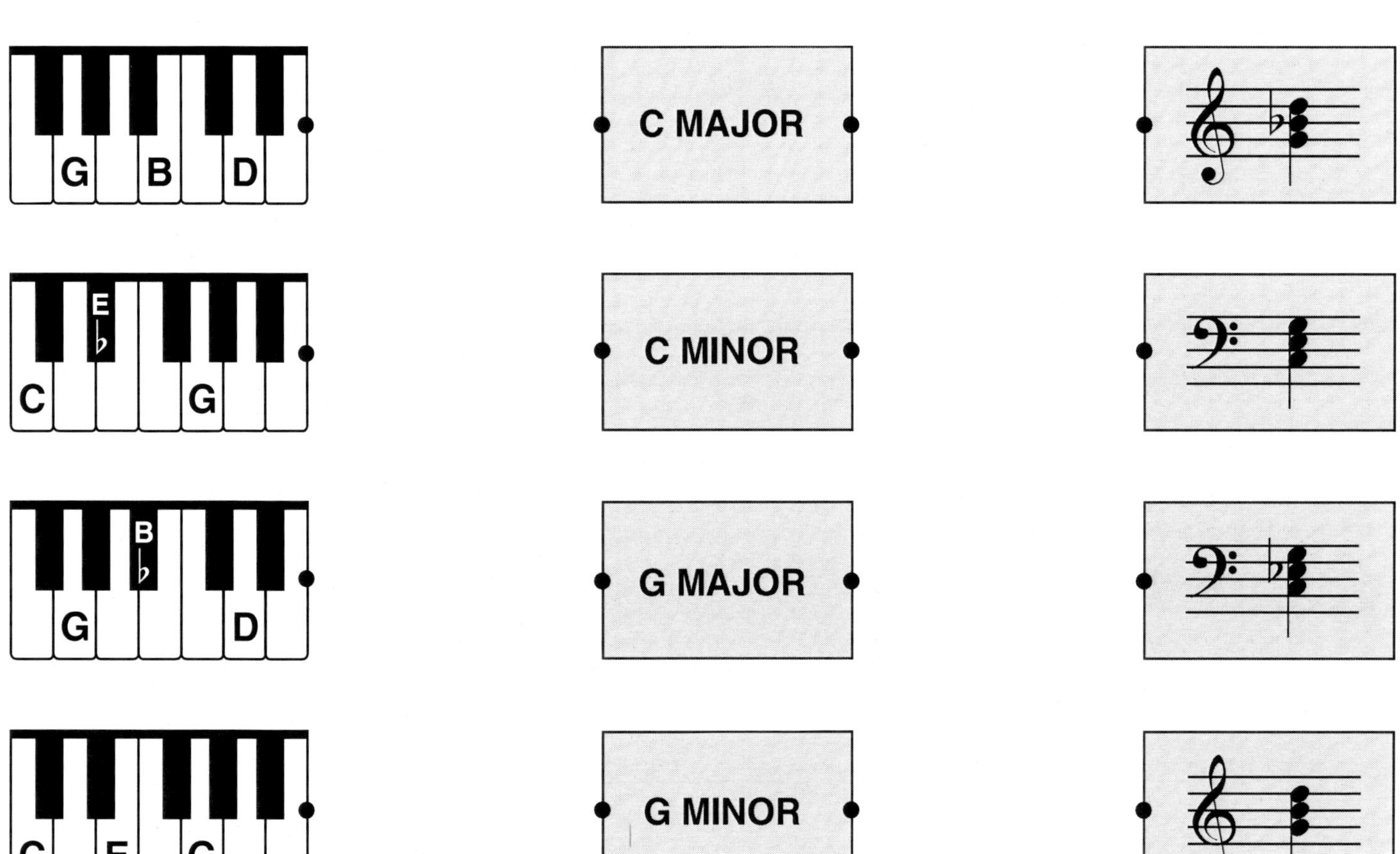

Jumpin' Triads

Put a check (✓) above each major triad and an **X** above each minor triad in *JUMPIN' TRIADS.*

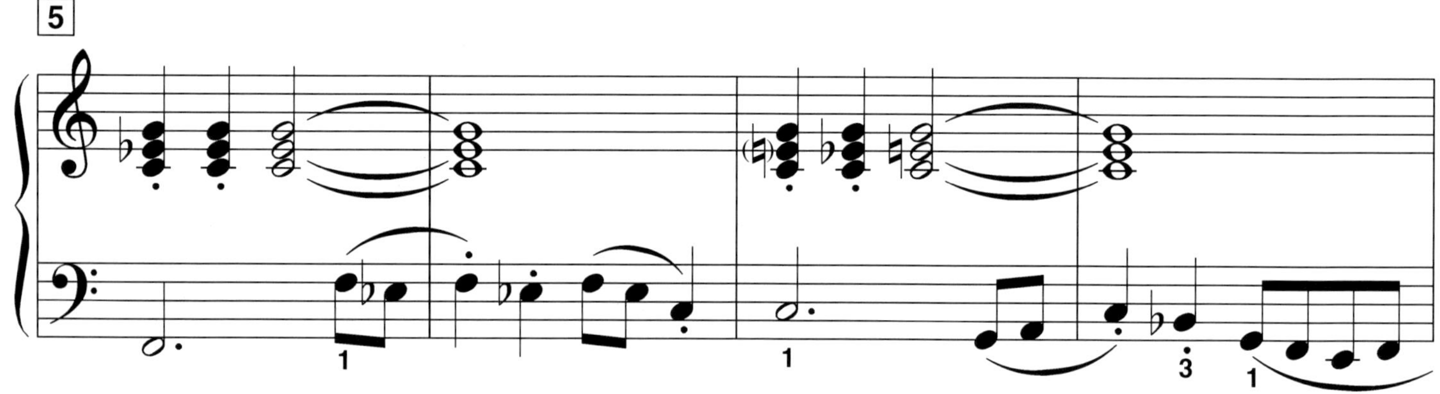

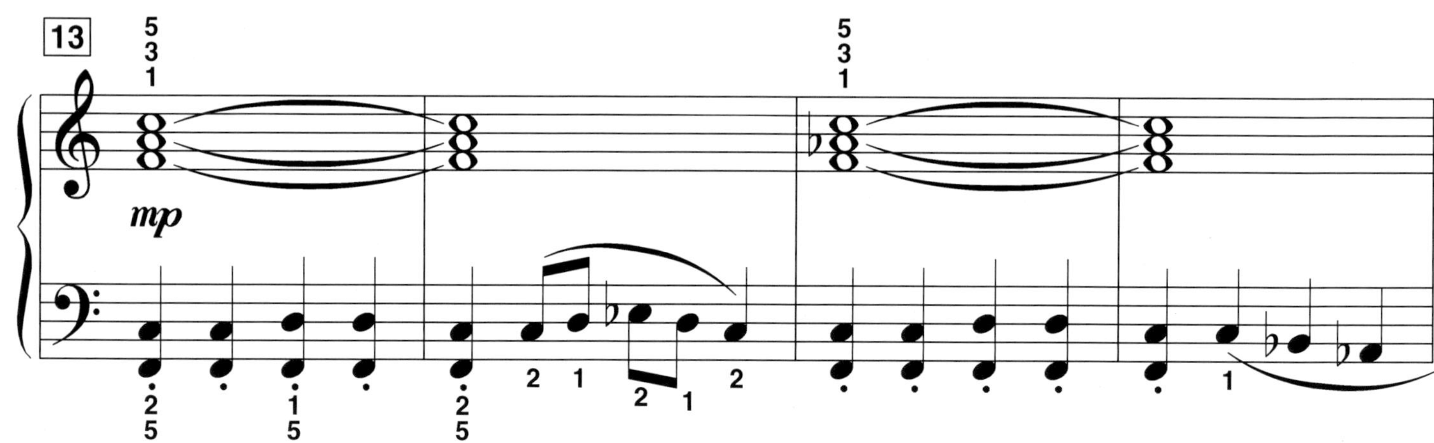

17
5
3
1
5
3
1
5
3
1
5
4
1
rit.
3-1
5
1
3
a tempo
21
5
3
1
f
4
3
1
25
1
1
3
1
29
rit.
mf
1
3
5
5
2
1
5
2
1
p
1
5
1
5

Unit 8

Use after page 37.

Primary Triads—Key of A Minor

The PRIMARY TRIADS are built on the 1st, 4th and 5th notes of the HARMONIC MINOR scale. Since the triads built on the 1st and 4th notes are minor triads, lower case Roman numerals are used (**i** and **iv**). The triad built on the 5th note is a major triad, so an upper case Roman numeral is used (**V**).

Primary Triads in the Key of A Minor

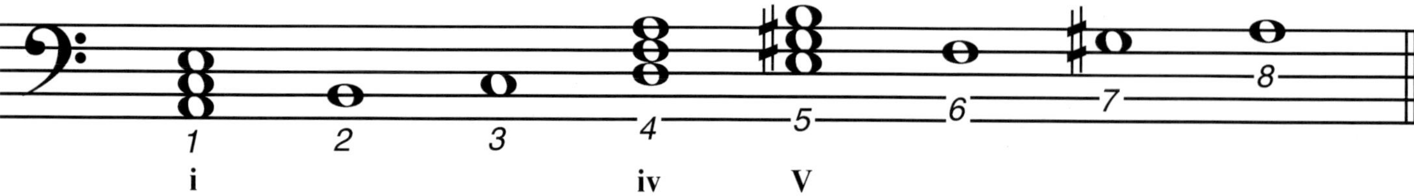

In the KEY OF A MINOR, the PRIMARY TRIADS are built on the notes: _____ _____ and _____ .
i **iv** **V**

On the keyboards below, write the letter names for the notes of the primary triads in the key of A minor.

i Chord

iv Chord

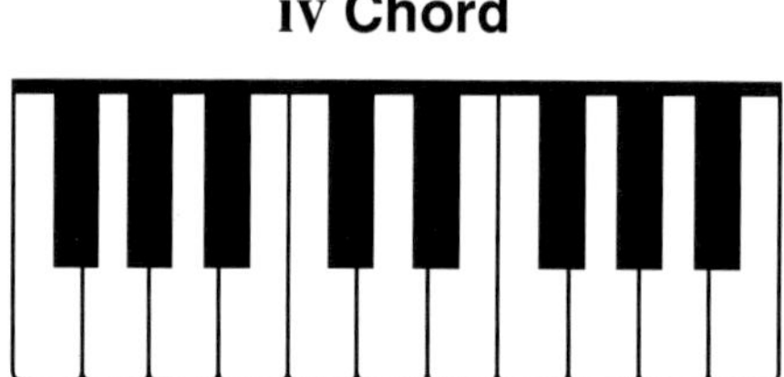

V Chord

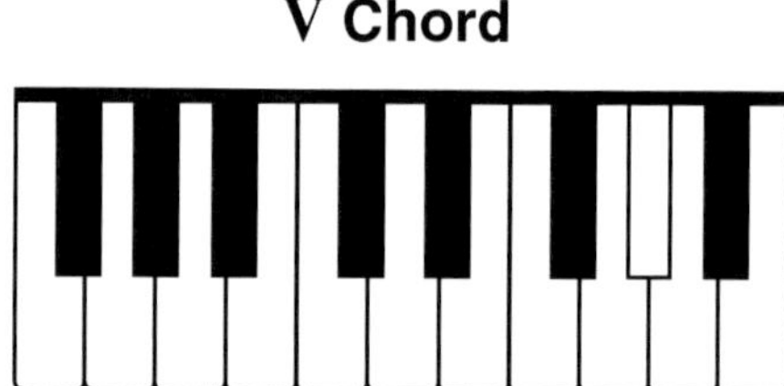

In the boxes below, write the letter names of the notes of the triad.
On the top line below the staff, write the Roman numeral name of the triad in the key of A minor.
On the bottom line, write the letter name of the chord. Write a small m for each minor triad; a large M for the major triad.

Letter Names:

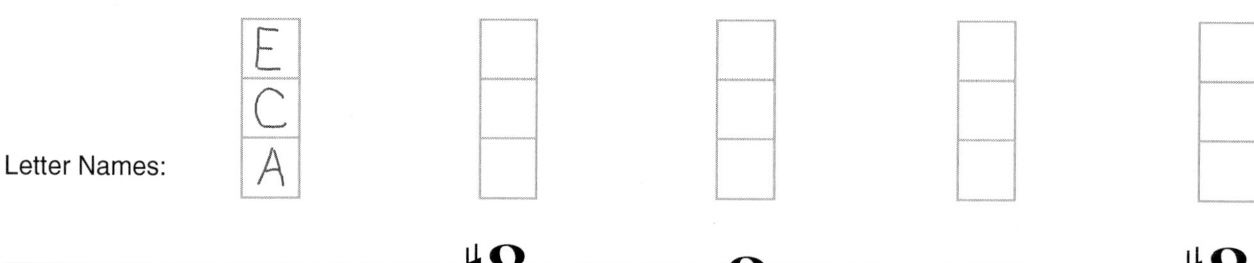

Roman Numeral: i _____ _____ _____ _____

Chord Name: Am _____ _____ _____ _____

A Minor Chord Progression

Primary Chords

To make playing the **i**, **iv** and **V** (or V^7) chords smoother moving from one to the other, the notes may be rearranged. The same notes must be used, but they may be played in different octaves.

IN ROOT POSITION | **SMOOTHER CHORD PROGRESSION**

The **i** chord (A minor chord) stays the same.

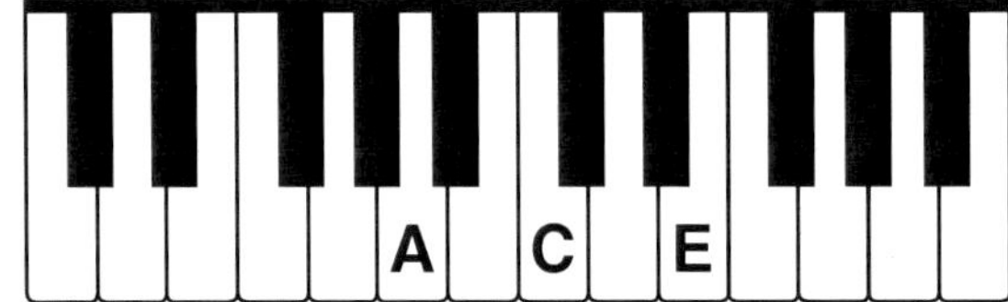

The top note (A) of the **iv** chord (D minor chord) is moved down an octave.

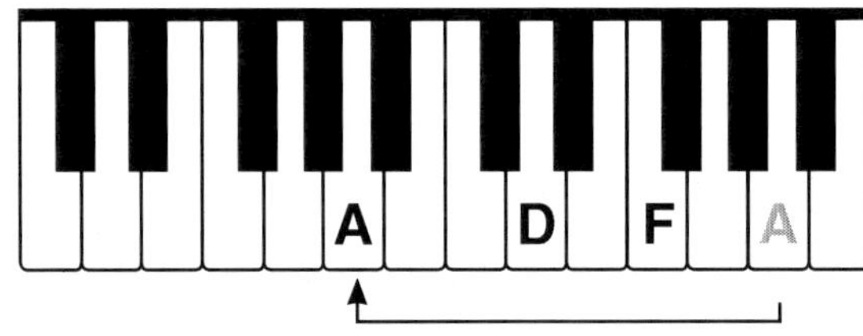

To make the V^7 chord (E^7 chord), first add the 7th tone (D) to the **V** chord (E chord). Move the root (E) up an octave, and leave out the 5th (B).

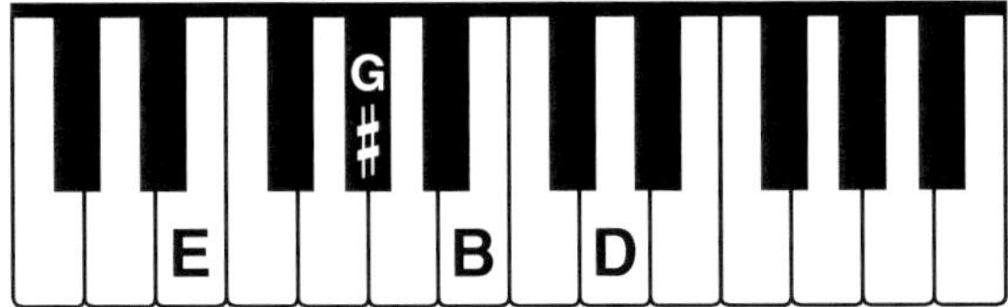

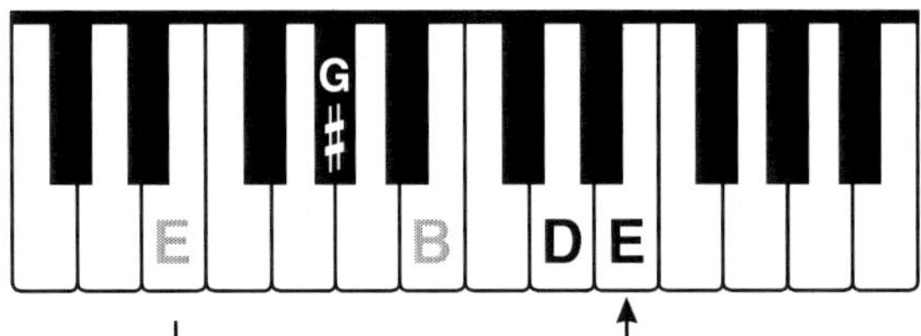

Play these examples of root position chords and the smoother chord progression.

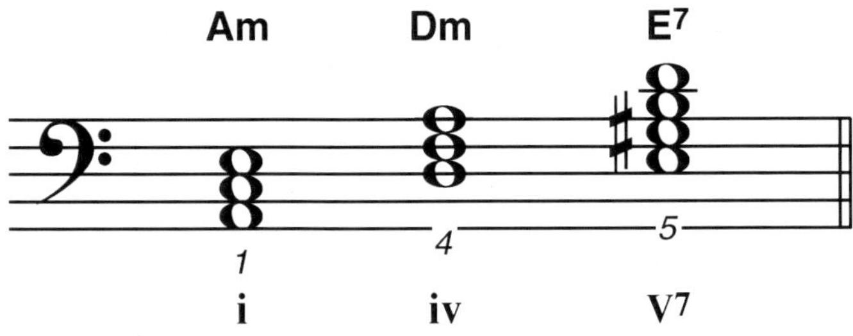

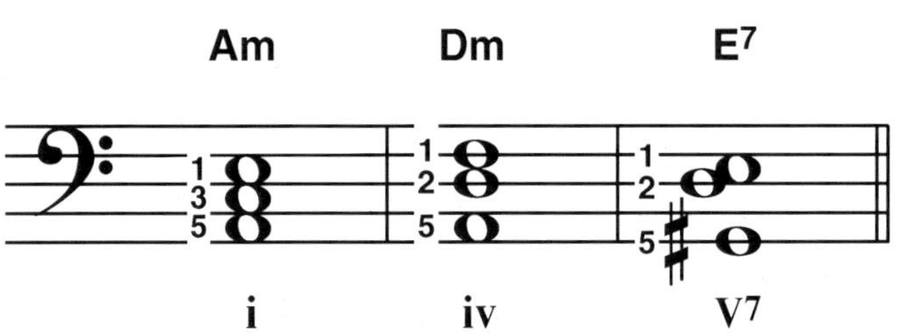

Write the correct Roman numeral on the line below the following chords from the key of A minor.

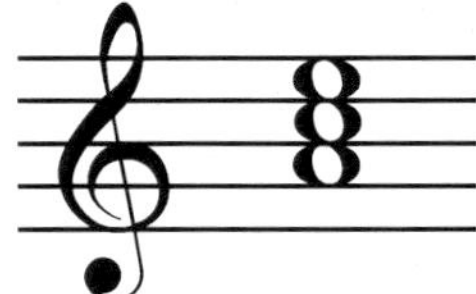

____ ____ ____

Memories of Yesterday

On each line below the chords (broken and block), write the Roman numeral name of the chord.

Andante moderato

Martha Mier

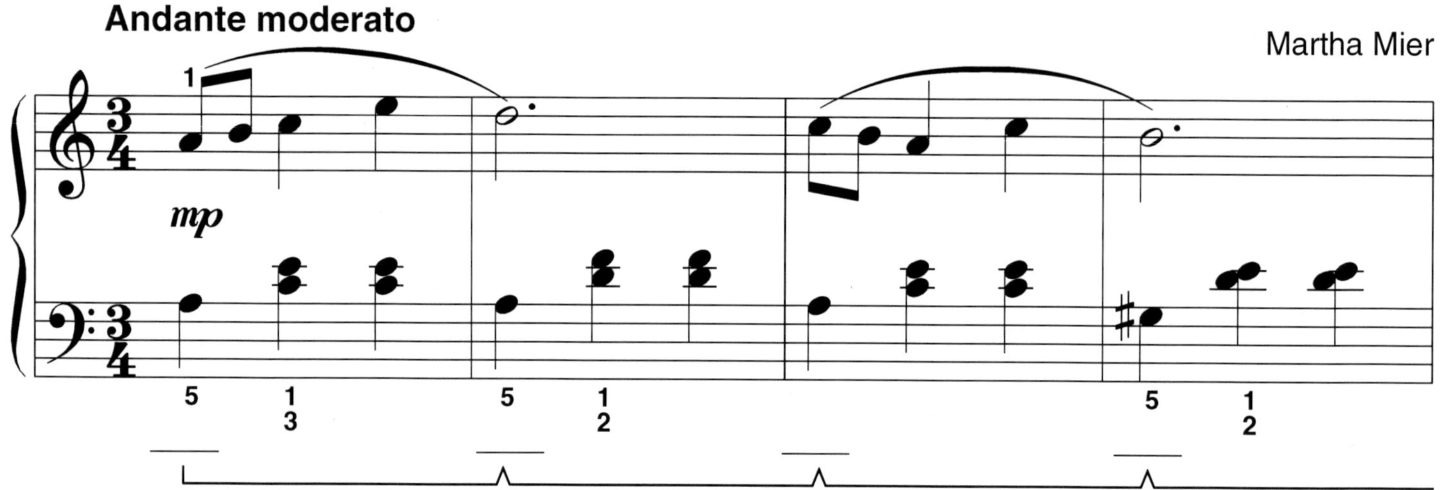

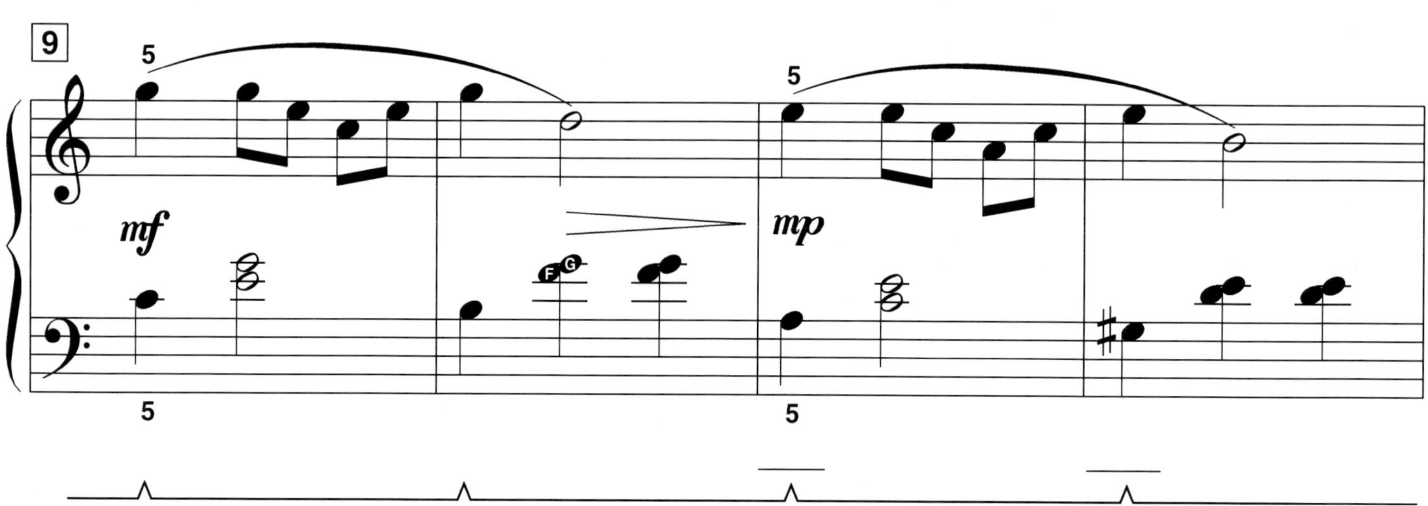

13
18
23
28
mp
mf
rit.
p

Unit 9

Use after page 39.

The Key of D Minor
(Relative of F Major)

Remember: Each major key has a RELATIVE MINOR key. It is called "relative" because it has the same key signature as the major key.

HOW TO FIND THE RELATIVE MINOR SCALE
The relative minor scale begins on the *6th tone* of the major scale, for example:

F MAJOR SCALE

D MINOR SCALE

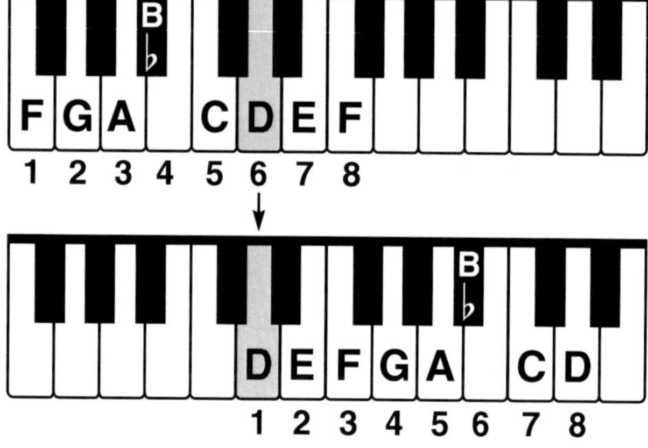

THE THREE KINDS OF MINOR SCALES

1. The NATURAL MINOR SCALE
   This scale uses the tones of the relative major scale.

2. The HARMONIC MINOR SCALE
   The 7th tone (C) is raised one half step, ascending and descending.

3. The MELODIC MINOR SCALE
   In the *ascending* scale, the 6th (B♭) and 7th (C) tones are raised one half step.

The *descending* scale is the same as the natural minor.

Ascending →

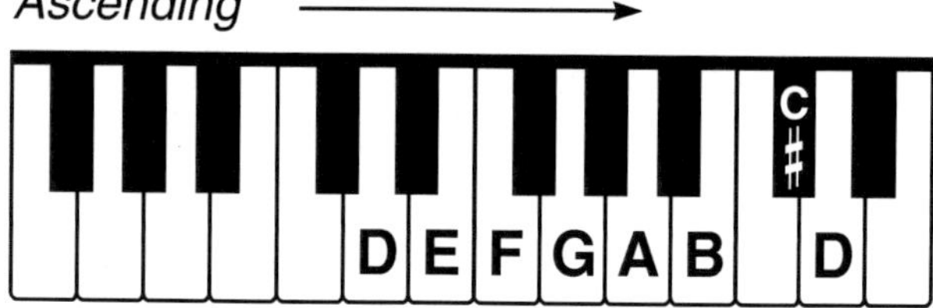

← *Descending*

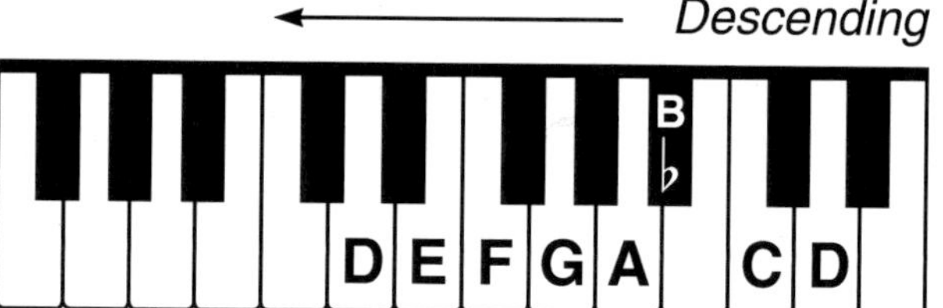

1. Play the following scales. Fill in the name of each scale (natural, harmonic or melodic).

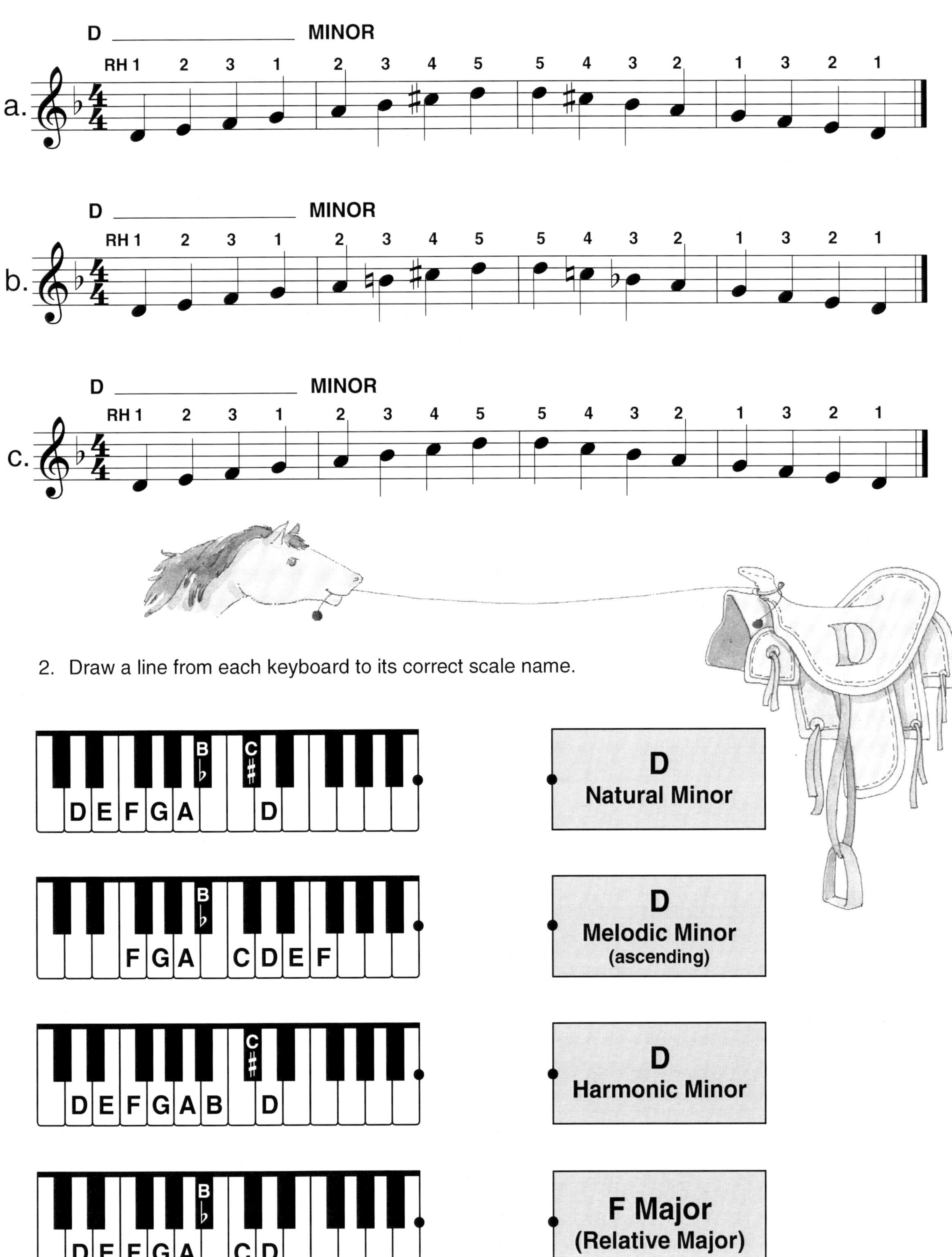

Wild Pony Roundup

Circle each D minor scale in *WILD PONY ROUNDUP.*

Martha Mier

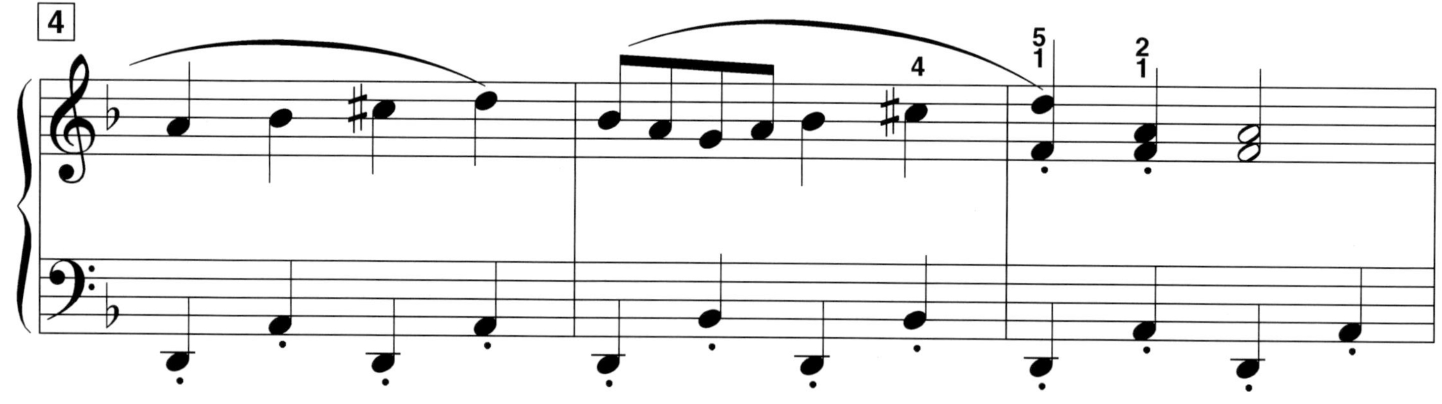

mp
mf
f
mf
f
rit.
ff

Unit 10

Use after page 41.

Primary Triads—Key of D Minor

Remember: The PRIMARY TRIADS are built on the 1st, 4th and 5th notes of the HARMONIC MINOR scale. Since the triads built on the 1st and 4th notes are minor triads, lower case Roman numerals are used (**i** and **iv**). The triad built on the 5th note is a major triad, so an upper case Roman numeral is used (**V**).

Primary Triads in the Key of D Minor

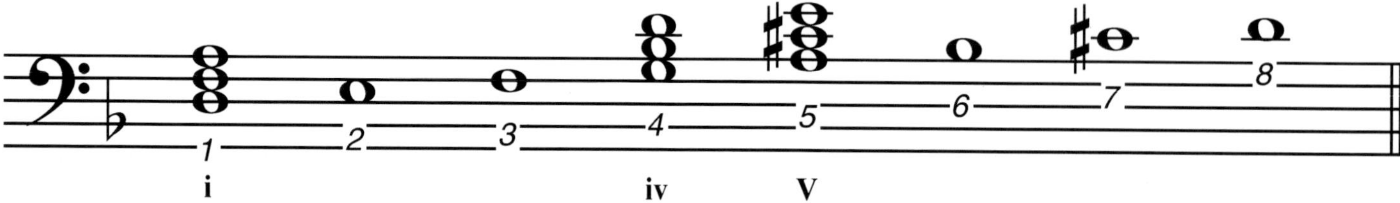

In the KEY OF D MINOR, the PRIMARY TRIADS are built on the notes: ____ ____ and ____ .
i iv V

On the keyboards below, write the letter names for the notes of the primary triads in the key of D minor.

i Chord

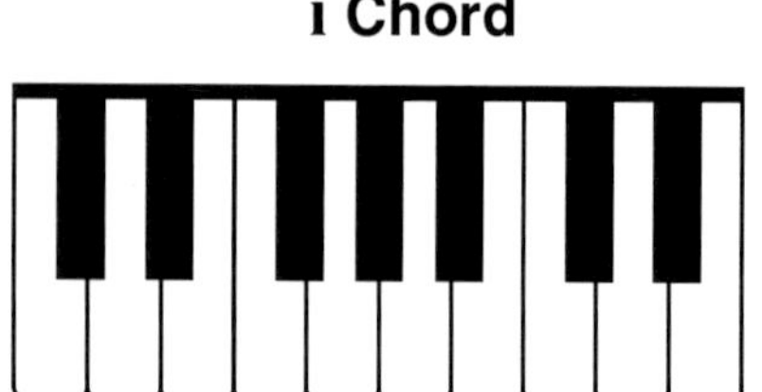

iv Chord

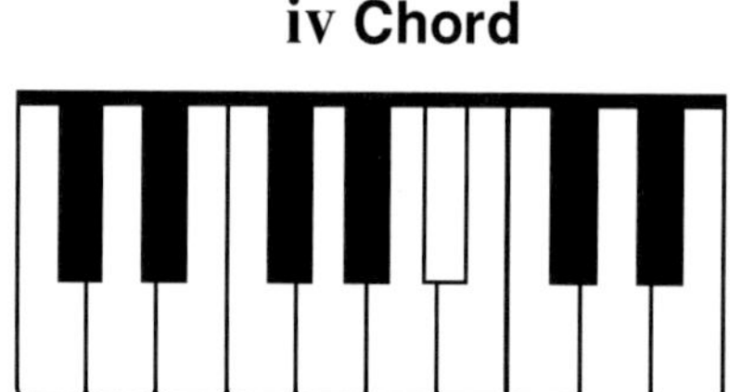

V Chord

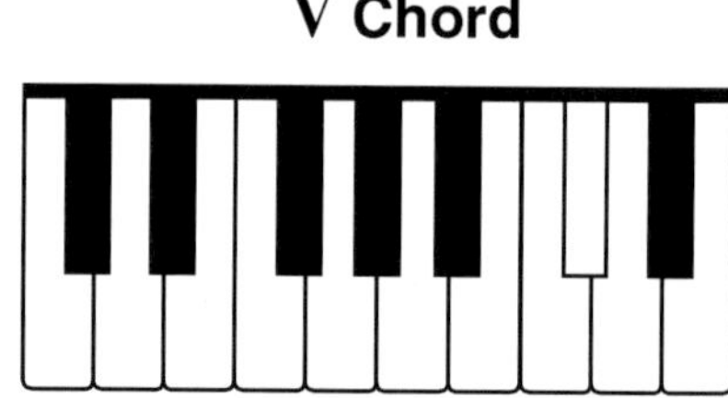

In the boxes below, write the letter names of the notes of the triad.
On the top line below the staff, write the Roman numeral name of the triad in the key of D minor.
On the bottom line, write the letter name of the chord. Write a small m for each minor triad; a large M for the major triad.

Letter Names: A F D

Roman Numeral: i ____ ____ ____ ____

Chord Name: Dm ____ ____ ____ ____

D Minor Chord Progression

Primary Chords

To make playing the **i**, **iv** and **V** (or V^7) chords smoother moving from one to the other, the notes may be rearranged. The same notes must be used, but they may be played in different octaves.

IN ROOT POSITION | **SMOOTHER CHORD PROGRESSION**

The **i** chord (D minor chord) stays the same.

The top note (D) of the **iv** chord (G minor chord) is moved down an octave.

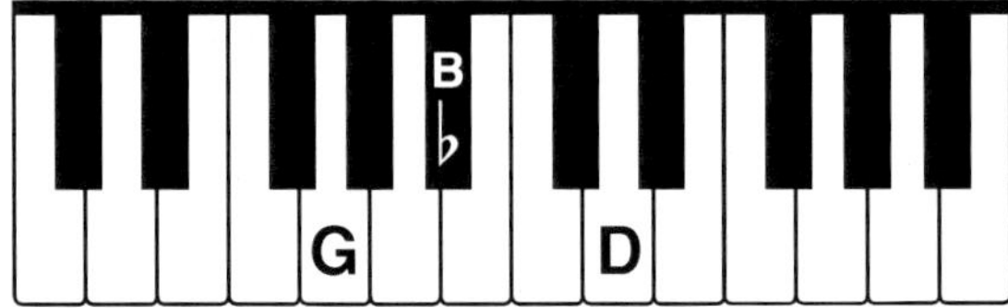

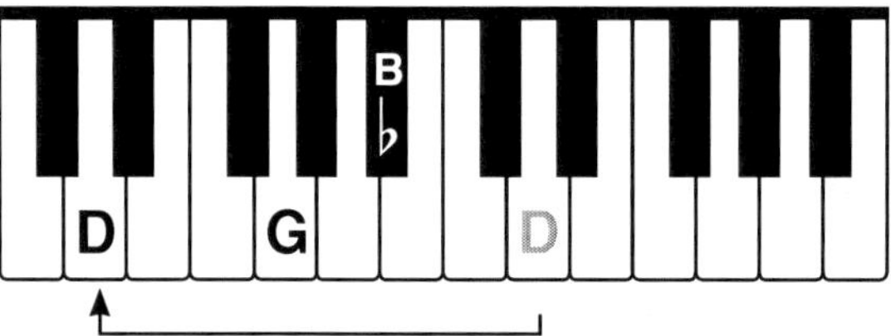

To make the V^7 chord (A^7 chord), first add the 7th tone (G) to the **V** chord (A chord). Move the root (A) up an octave, and leave out the 5th (E).

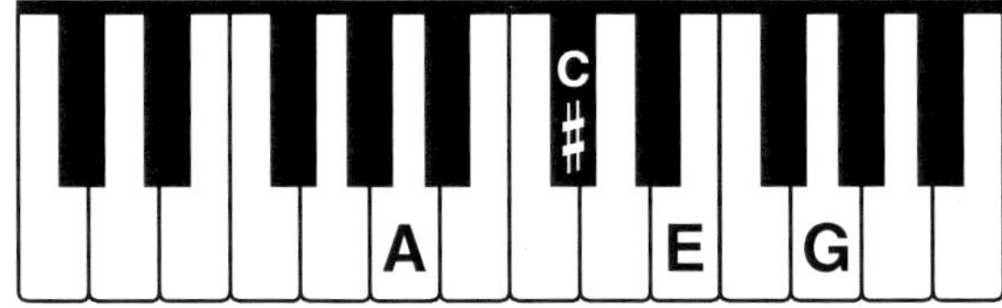

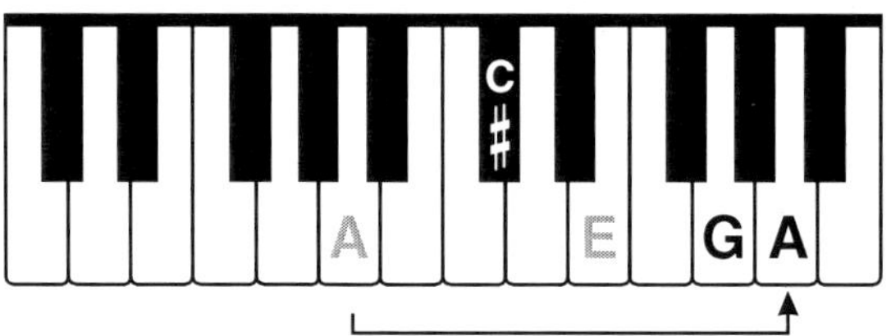

Play these examples of root position chords and the smoother chord progression.

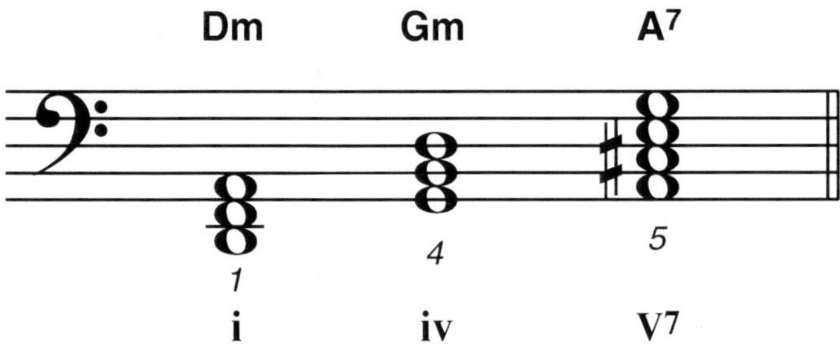

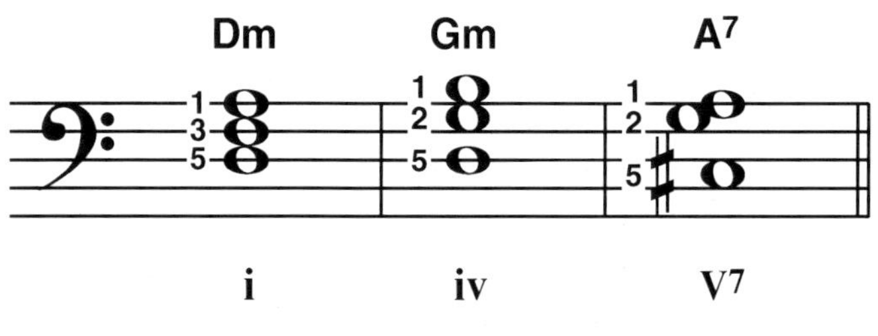

Write the correct Roman numeral on the line below the following chords from the key of A minor.

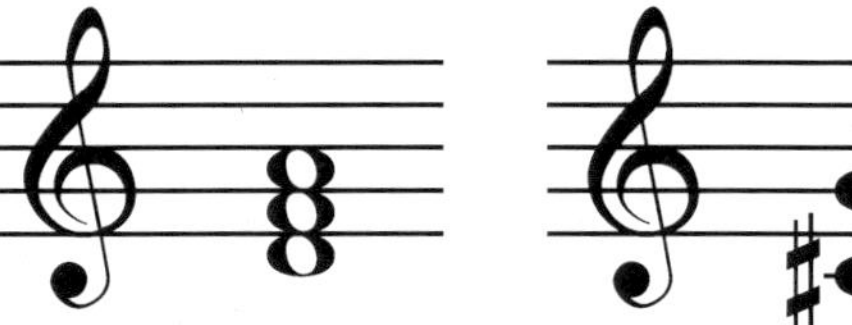

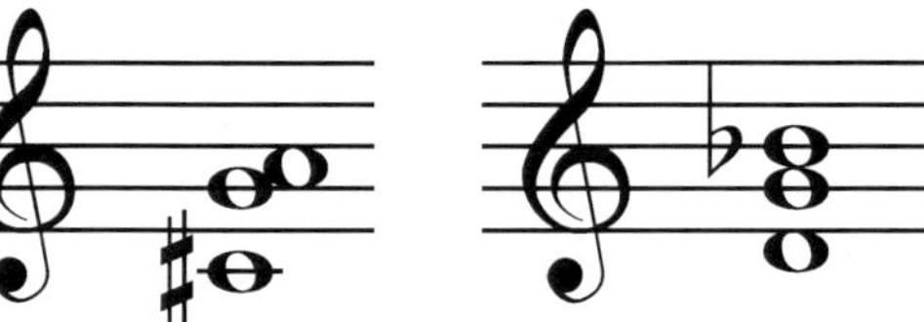

Greek Folk Dance

On each line below the chords (broken and block), write the Roman numeral name of the chord.

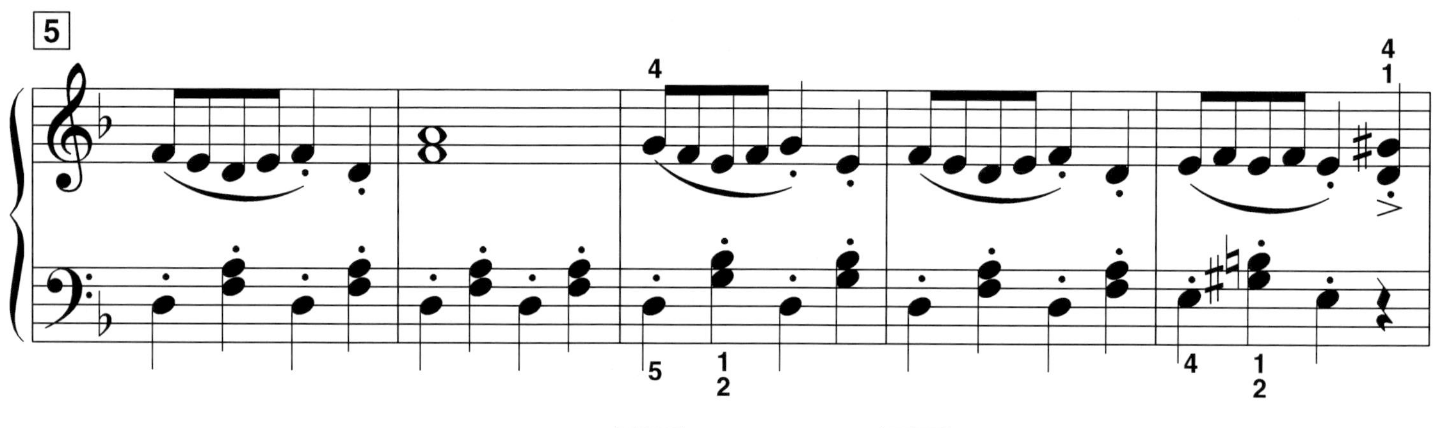

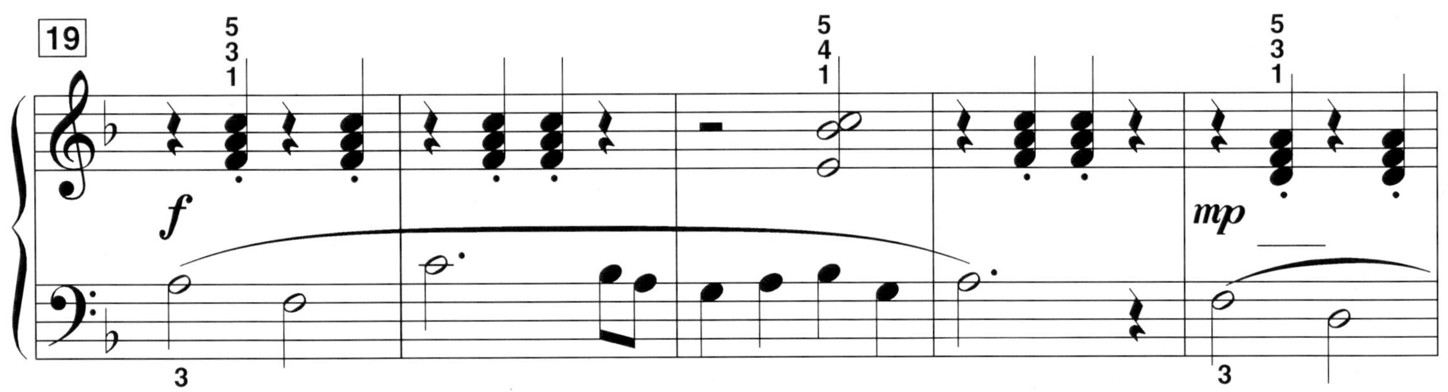
19
5
3
1
5
4
1
5
3
1
f
mp
3
3

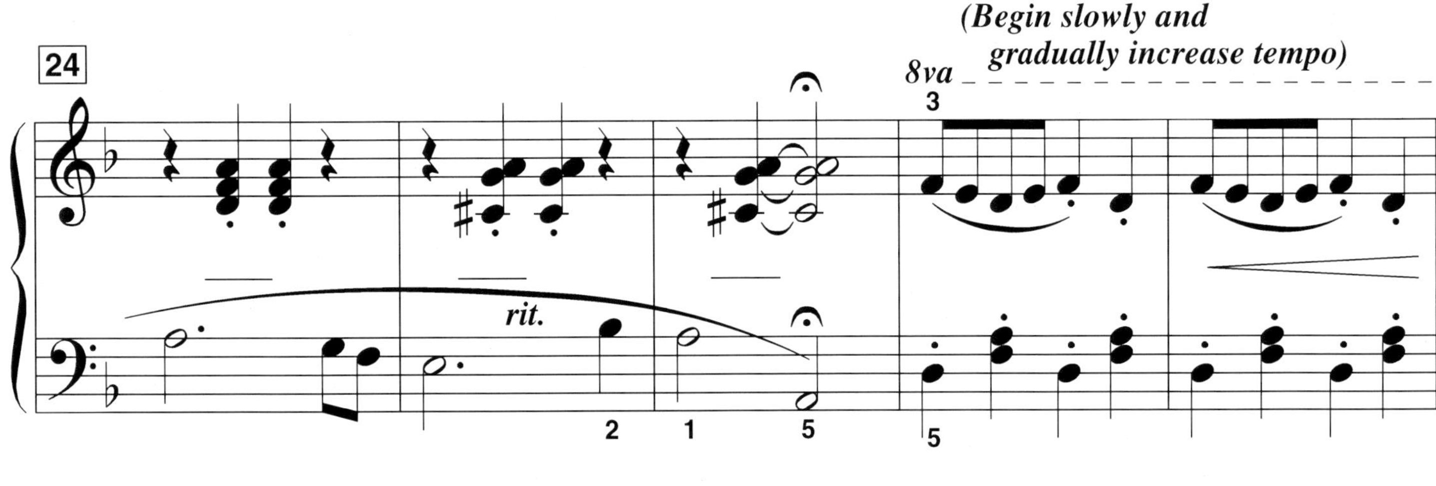
24
(Begin slowly and
gradually increase tempo)
8va
3
rit.
2
1
5
5

29
(8va)
a tempo
3
mf
f

34
(8va)
loco
3
mp
2 1
3 1
4
f

Unit 11

Use after page 45.

New Time Signatures

3/8	means **3** beats to each measure. means an **eighth note** gets one beat.

6/8	means **6** beats to each measure. means an **eighth note** gets one beat.

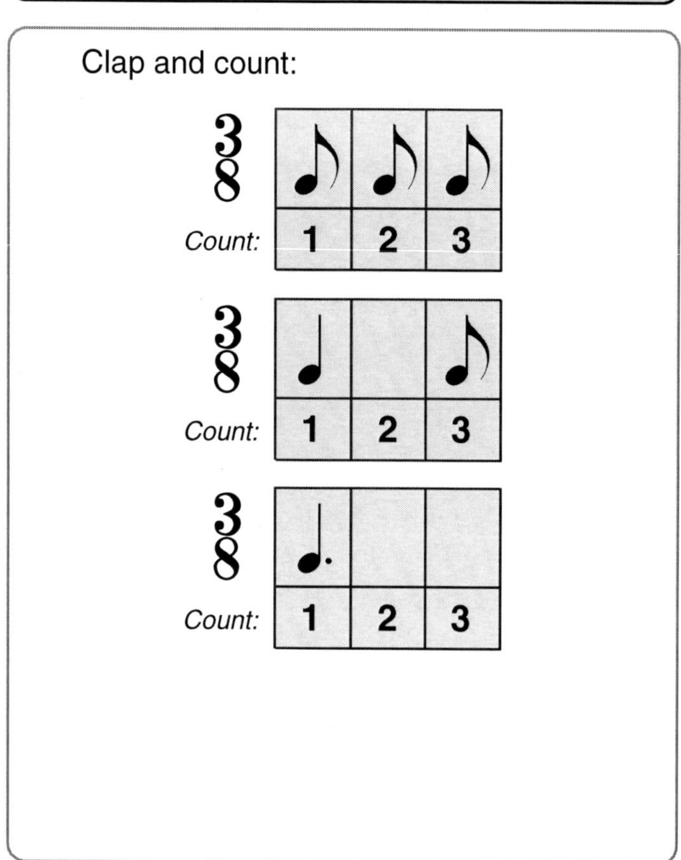

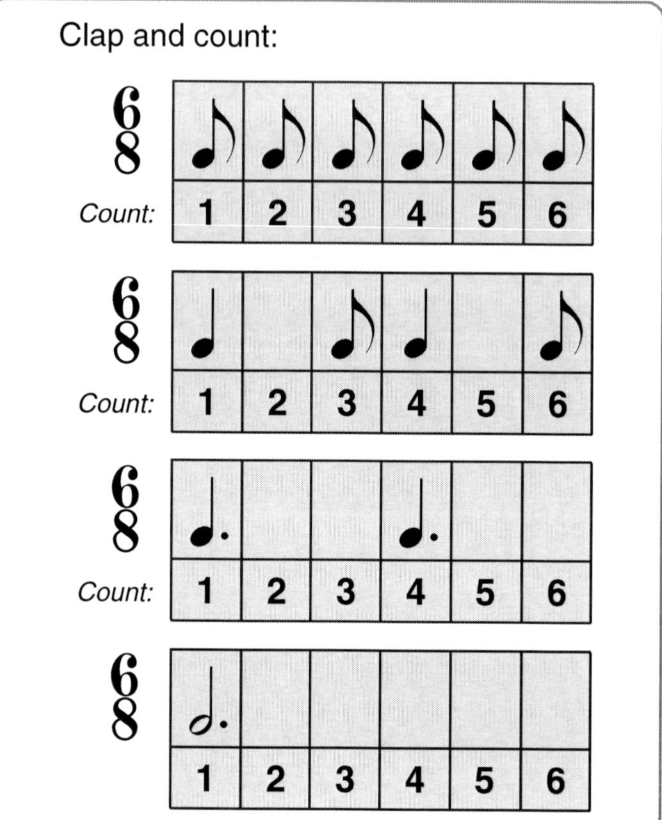

1. Write the number of beats each note receives in 3/8 time.

2. Write the number of beats each note receives in 6/8 time.

3. Tap each example on a table top and count aloud.

1. In each measure of this piece there is one error related to 6/8 time. Find and correct the errors. Play the piece.

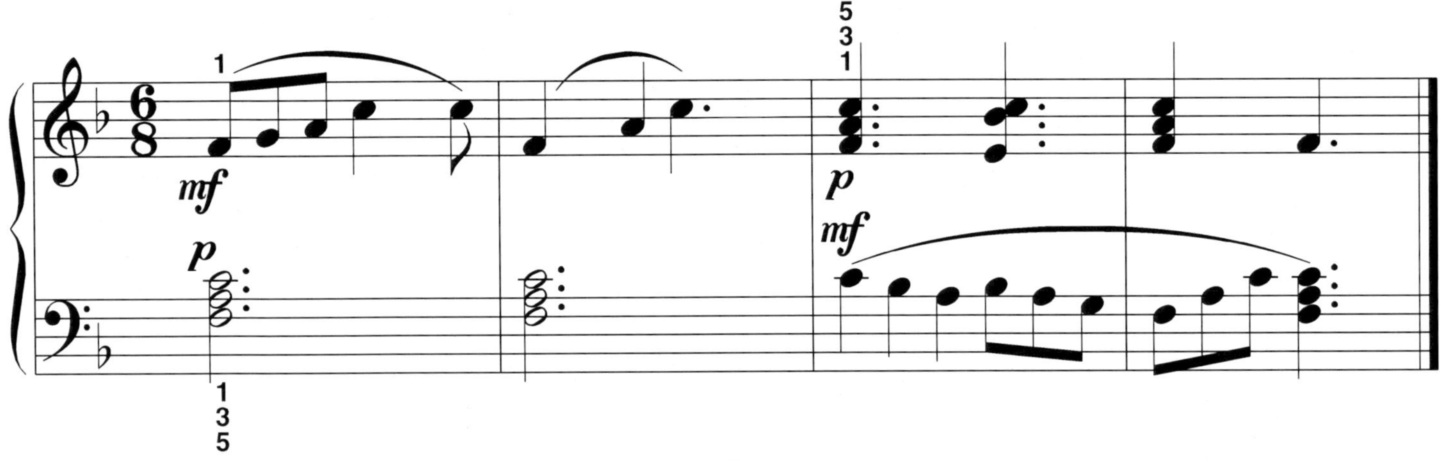

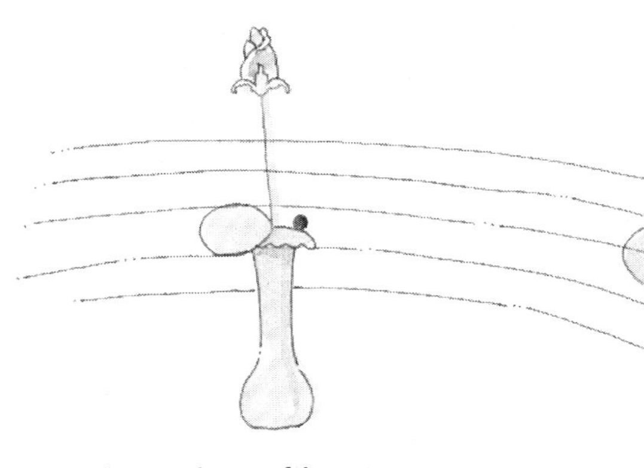

2. For each example below, add the total number of beats that the notes would receive in 6/8 time and write the number on the line.

a. ♩ + ♩. + ♪ = _____ beats

b. ♪ + ♪ + ♪ = _____ beats

c. ♩. + ♩. + ♩. = _____ beats

d. ♪ + 𝅗𝅥. + ♪ = _____ beats

e. 𝅗𝅥. + ♩. + 𝅗𝅥. = _____ beats

f. ♩ + ♪ + ♩ = _____ beats

g. ♩ + 𝅗𝅥. + ♩ = _____ beats

Basket of Roses

In each measure of *BASKET OF ROSES,* write the counts (1-2-3) under the staff.

Andante moderato

Martha Mier

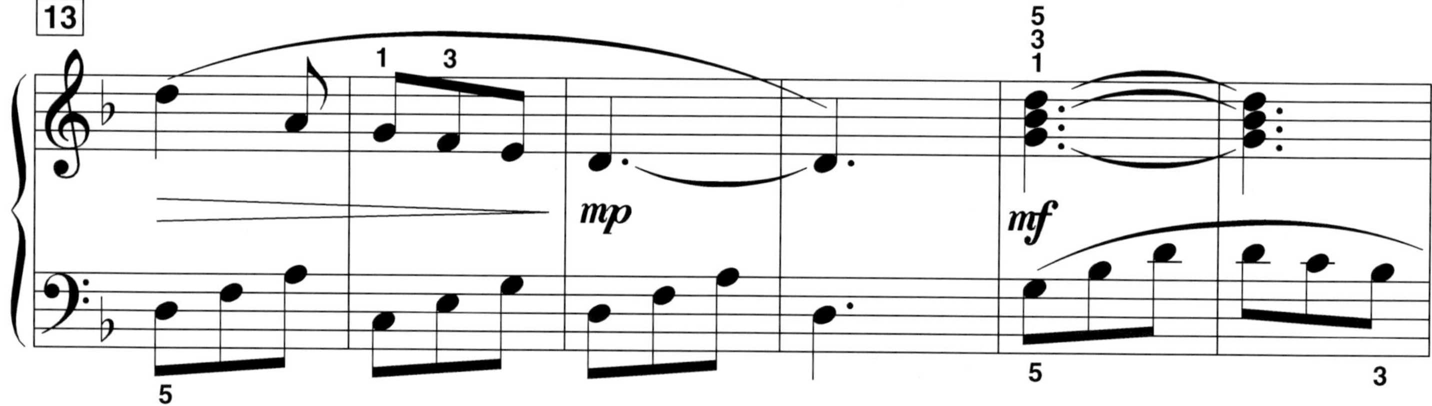

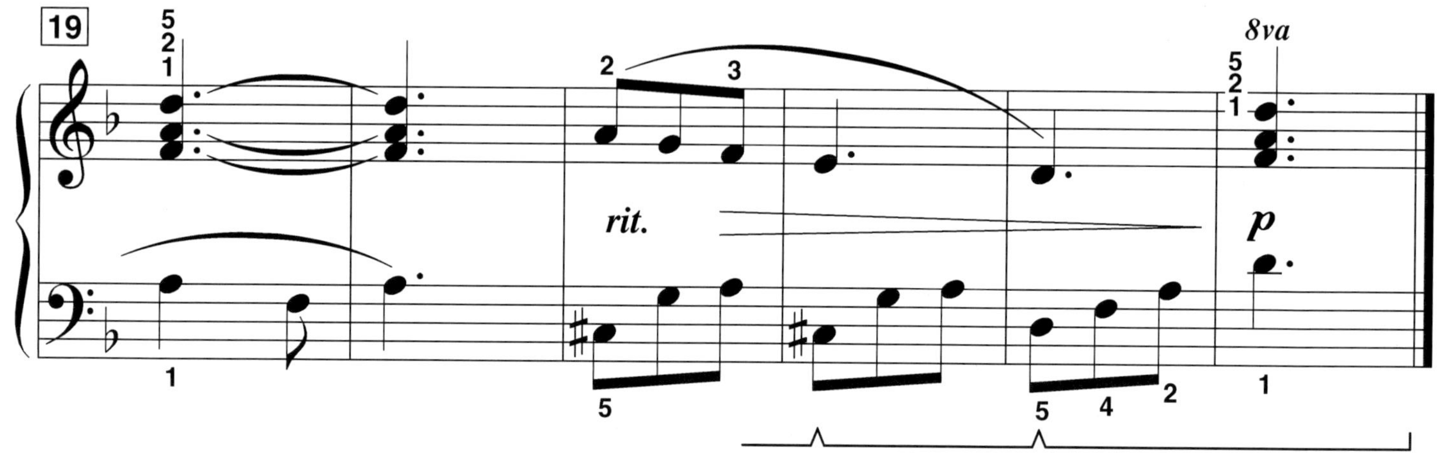

The Chase

In each measure of *THE CHASE,* write the counts (1-2-3-4-5-6) under the staff.

Martha Mier

Allegro

2nd time RH 8va

mp *mf–p*

1 3 5

5

1 2

9

2 1 3 2

1. 2.

(8va) *loco*

mf LH 2

13

RH 2 RH 2 2 2

5 1

f *rit.*

Review Worksheet

Major and Minor Triads

On the banner of each hot-air ballon, write the name of the major or minor triad.

Review Worksheet

Primary Chords and Scales

Draw a line from the primary chords and scales to the matching sailboat.

1. 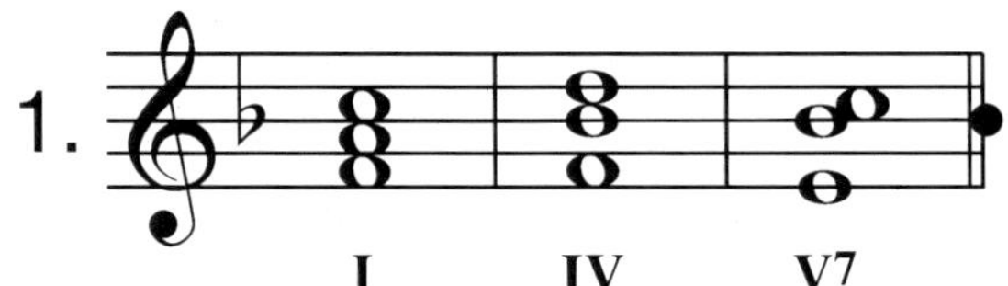

2. 

3. 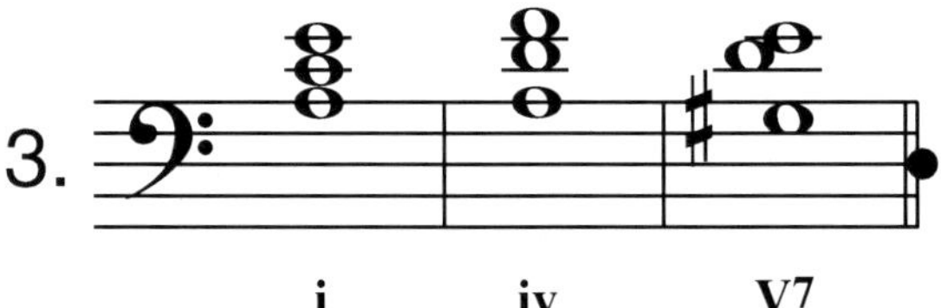

4. 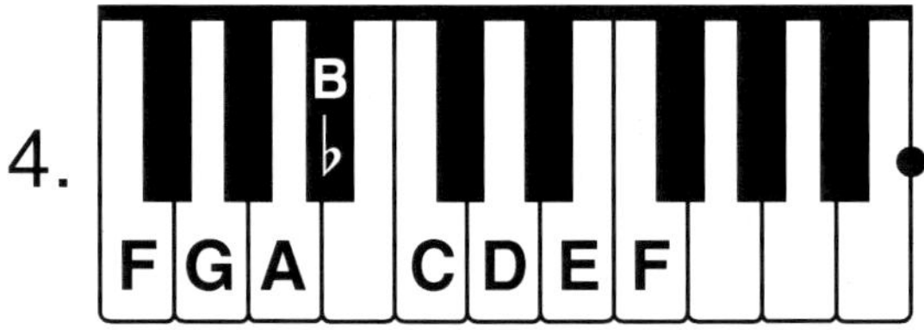

5. 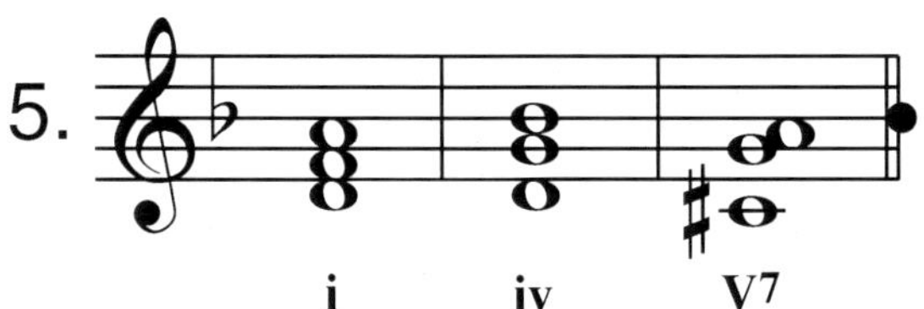

6. 

7. 

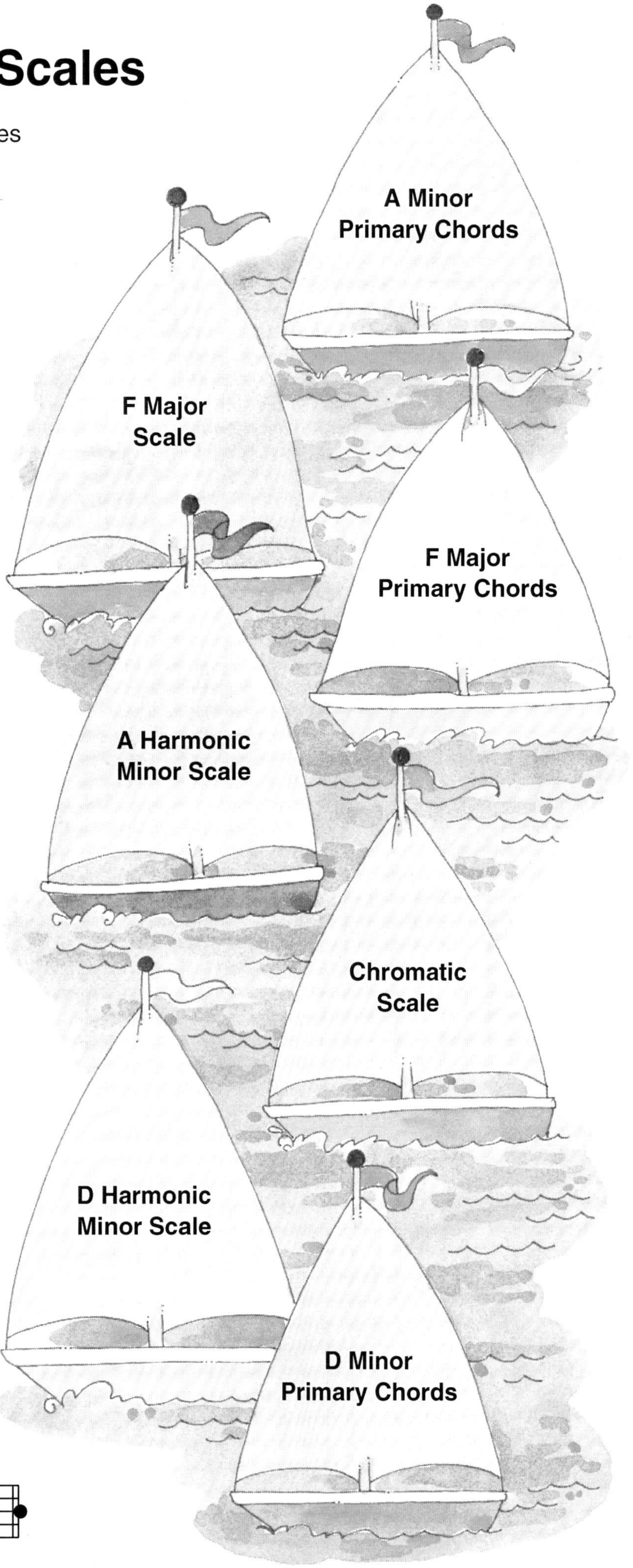

A Minor Primary Chords

F Major Scale

F Major Primary Chords

A Harmonic Minor Scale

Chromatic Scale

D Harmonic Minor Scale

D Minor Primary Chords

Crossword Puzzle

Complete the sentences below, then solve the crossword puzzle.

DOWN

1. The ____________________ scale is made up entirely of HALF STEPS.
4. These chords (I IV V7) are the ________________ chords in the key of F MAJOR.
5. This scale is the A ________________ minor scale.
6. In the ascending ____________ minor scale, the 6th and 7th tones are raised one half step.

ACROSS

2. A major triad consists of a ________________ , major 3rd and perfect 5th.
3. This scale is the D ______________________ minor scale.
7. Each key has a ________________________ minor key that has the same key signature as the major key.
8. A minor triad consists of a root, ________________ 3rd and perfect 5th.